A MATTER OF TWO CHINAS

The China-Taiwan Issue in U.S. Foreign Policy

William R. Kintner & John F. Copper

FOREIGN POLICY RESEARCH INSTITUTE
Philadelphia, Pennsylvania

WILLIAM R. KINTNER is President of the Foreign Policy Research Institute and Professor of Political Science, University of Pennsylvania. He was the United States Ambassador to Thailand in 1973-1975, served in the Korean War, and has traveled extensively in East Asia.

JOHN F. COPPER is Associate Professor in International Studies at Southwestern, Memphis. Previously a Research Fellow at the Hoover Institution on War, Revolution and Peace, Stanford University, and on the faculty of the University of Maryland, Far East Division, he has lived and traveled in Asia for more than ten years, residing in Taiwan for more than five years.

Library of Congress Cataloging in Publication Data

Kintner, William Roscoe, 1915–
  A matter of two Chinas.

  1. United States—Foreign relations—China.
  2. China—Foreign relations—United States.
  3. United States—Foreign relations—Taiwan.
  4. Taiwan—Foreign relations—United States.
I. Copper, John Franklin, joint author. II. Title.
E183.8.C5K565   327.73'051   79-4254

Foreign Policy Research Institute
3508 Market Street
Philadelphia, Pennsylvania 19104

FOREIGN POLICY RESEARCH INSTITUTE

Purpose

The Institute was founded in 1955 to:

EXAMINE international trends and fundamental issues facing American foreign policy.

PUBLISH U.S. foreign policy recommendations and studies that contribute to American security and a stable international order.

EDUCATE select young scholars in international relations for service in U.S. foreign policy and national security agencies, and as teachers in American educational institutions.

Program

To accomplish its purpose the Institute:

MAINTAINS a staff of specialists in the field of international relations and related disciplines.

PROVIDES facilities and services for these specialists, including an extensive library of books, periodicals and newspapers.

OFFERS additional access to expertise through the distinguished scholars on its Board of Research Consultants.

GRANTS graduate and undergraduate students opportunities to develop their talents and further their education for careers in the U.S. government, international business and the American educational system.

Presentation

The results of FPRI's research are presented in:

REPORTS fulfilling government contracts or special grants from foundations, corporations and individuals.

PUBLICATIONS, including ORBIS, FPRI's renowned quarterly journal of world affairs, a book series and occasional monographs.

CONFERENCES for policymakers, scholars and interested citizens. These efforts ensure that the Institute's work reaches public policymakers, scholars, business people and other concerned citizens.

Foreign Policy Research Institute is a publicly supported, nonprofit, tax-exempt corporation as described in Section 170 (b)(1)(A)(vi) of the Internal Revenue Code. All contributions to the Institute are tax deductible.

CONTENTS

Preface   vii

Introduction   1

1   Political-Military Implications of the New China Policy   5

2   The Economic Basis of U.S. China Policy   21

3   The Legal Dimensions of U.S. China Policy   39

4   Human Rights: "The Soul of American Foreign Policy"   63

5   Taiwan's Options and U.S. China Policy   79

6   The United States and the Future of Taiwan   93

Appendix A: Mutual Defense Treaty Between the United States and the Republic of China (1954)   103

Appendix B: The Shanghai Communique (1972)   107

Appendix C: Joint Communique on the Establishment of Diplomatic Relations Between the United States and the People's Republic of China (1978)   113

Notes   115

PREFACE

The idea of writing about the reality of two Chinas has been in the minds of both authors for several years. America's recent recognition of the People's Republic of China and the derecognition of the Republic of China make it all the more important that the matter of two Chinas be better understood. This book has been written toward that end.

The authors wish to express their appreciation to all who contributed to this work. We have benefited from the advice and comments of many individuals associated with the Foreign Policy Research Institute beginning with its founder and current Diplomat-in-Residence, Ambassador Robert Strausz-Hupé. Special gratitude is owed Lyu-shun Shen for his invaluable research assistance. Our thanks also to Alan H. Luxenberg, Charles B. Purrenhage, and Patrick E. Graupp for their assistance in the production of this book. Our competent secretarial, typist and production staff have done yeoman work in deciphering handwriting that borders on hieroglyphics and producing draft chapters for subsequent honing. For their contribution to this taxing process we pay tribute to Dorothy Greenwood, Carmena Pyfrom, Donna Reese, Sandy Bailey, Dorothy Stephens, Josephine Fabrizio and Carmela Gioffre.

The views expressed in this book, however, along with its deficiencies, belong to the authors and it is with them that the responsibility for receiving suggestions or criticisms belongs.

William R. Kintner and John F. Copper
Philadelphia
March 1979

INTRODUCTION

On December 15, 1978 President Carter announced that the United States would establish formal diplomatic relations with the People's Republic of China, effective January 1, and that ambassadors would be exchanged in March. He also gave notice that the United States Defense Pact with the Republic of China (ROC) on Taiwan would end at the close of 1979. These moves, said the President, had no other purpose than "the advancement of peace."

If Carter's action surprised the country, the country's reaction surprised the Administration. Responding to public pressure, Democrats and Republicans displayed a rare unanimity in criticizing aspects of the President's decision and insisting that Taiwanese security be reinforced by more than pious reliance on Peking's goodwill. Normalization, Carter style, undoubtedly ran against the grain of Congressional sentiment and public opinion. In mid-summer 1978, both the U.S. Senate and House resolved that the President should consult Congress before terminating the U.S.-Republic of China Mutual Defense Treaty. Public opinion polls indicated that the American public by a majority of more than three to one opposed the United States' breaking diplomatic relations with Taipei *in order to establish ties with Peking.* They also opposed terminating the defense pact with the ROC by a like majority. Newspaper editorials and the cautious attitude of most scholars writing on the subject reflected these attitudes.

The President's position was complicated by what were obvious violations of his own celebrated diplomatic standards—openness and consultation. [1] Important legal and human rights questions raised by normalization were given additional force by a certain sloppiness in the details concerning the future security of Taiwan. Despite assertions by the Administration that the United States would sell arms to Taipei after the termination of the Mutual Defense Treaty, Chinese Communist Party Chairman Hua Kuo-feng warned that "after the normalization, the continued sale of arms to Taiwan by the United States does not conform to the principles of the normalization." The Administration's insistence that this protest was simply *pro forma* was undercut by its admission that written assurances from Peking not to attack Taiwan had never been sought. [2]

The President's initiative was marred further by suspicions of political expediency. Some observers speculated that "normalization" was a substitute for Carter's frustration in other areas: the Egyptian-Israeli peace talks had stalled and the SALT negotiations were winding too slowly towards their conclusion. Others believed that the timing enabled the Administration to avoid strong Congressional reaction, taking place as it did just after the Congressional elections when the Congress itself was not in session.

Administration explanations for "normalization" differed, depending upon the identity of the spokesman. Two well-defined groups seem to have influenced Carter's China policy. For one, recognition of Peking constitutes a means of gaining leverage over the Soviet Union. This group perceives that the sustained Soviet arms build-up is shifting the balance of power against the United States. Thus the United States must ally with the People's Republic of China. They also argued that the existing Sino-American detente was fragile and that without further normalization it might deteriorate, possibly leading to a Sino-Soviet rapprochement.

The other group sees American ties with Peking as the critical ingredient to the establishment of long-term stability in East Asia. Such stability would enable the United States to "lower its profile" still further: the withdrawal of American troops from Korea could be accomplished with less danger, and the U.S. military presence in Asia could be reduced.

2

The regional and strategic arguments of the two groups seem to have been given critical impetus by events within China itself. The late 1978 wall-poster campaigns and the sudden re-emergence of Teng Hsiao-ping—seventy-four years old and twice purged—suggested some instability. Whether Washington's action represented U.S. thinking that Teng and his colleagues were the best long-term partners, whether Teng's group gained ascendancy before or after Carter's actions, is uncertain. The relationship of U.S. recognition to internal Chinese politics is shrouded in mystery.

Washington's recognition of Peking thus raises critical issues that go beyond the act of exchanging ambassadors. Both U.S. leaders and the American people need to understand the political and strategic consequences of a closer association between the U.S. and the PRC. We must be able to assess the impact of normalization on the current international situation. This event should also be placed in the context of general American foreign policy objectives, both global and regional.

The intent of this book is to assess the implications of Carter's decision: (1) political-military; (2) economic; (3) legal; (4) human rights. Finally, Taiwan's future—a "new" country, an "independent" Chinese province, or an object of conquest for Peking—must be discussed, for it may very well determine the success or failure of America's China policy as well as its overall Asian strategy. In the final chapter we shall therefore suggest what the United States might do to assure the well-being of Taiwan during the initial "post-recognition" period.

Chapter One
POLITICAL-MILITARY IMPLICATIONS OF THE NEW CHINA POLICY

President Carter's recognition of the People's Republic of China was a many-sided act. It could be seen as a logical step on the road to U.S.-PRC rapprochement begun nearly a decade ago, after a long period of unremitting hostility. A closer relationship between the world's most powerful industrial state and the world's most populous country suggested the grand sweep of an historical change in the balance of power. In Asia itself, it marked one more break with the post-World War II American-sponsored security system, founded on American protection of a disarmed Japan, alliances with the smaller mainland states, and containment of communism.

The rapprochement between the United States and the People's Republic, and recognition itself, must be assessed in the strategic context of U.S. policy over the last decade. The paramount characteristic of this policy has been Washington's attempt to fashion a new and less tense relationship with Moscow: more emphasis on negotiations, less on force. Washington's "opening" to Peking dates from the earliest phase of U.S.-Soviet detente, and the Sino-Soviet dispute provided the crucial context for Nixon's historic trip to Peking in 1972.

In retrospect, it is tempting to see the Nixon overture as a simple act of balance of power politics: the United States, its strength ebbing because of Vietnam, seeks the PRC as a counter to the Soviet Union, while the PRC, fearful of Soviet antagonism to China, wants American help in deterring Moscow. But the vital regional purposes of the United States must be kept in mind. Washington's reconsideration of its Asian possibilities required a drastic revision of its responsibilities toward the security arrangements in the Far East. Thus, the PRC offered not only a useful association that, if managed cordially, would redouble Soviet interest in better relations with the United States, but also the prospect of a responsible partner to stabilize war-torn Southeast Asia. The practical benefits could be easily reckoned: a diversion of Soviet military resources; a reduction of regional strife that might put remaining U.S. defense commitments to the test after Washington extricated itself from Vietnam.

These advantages could not be grasped, however, unless several delicate situations were managed simultaneously. One prerequisite was not to sacrifice U.S.-USSR relations to Sino-Soviet hostility, especially if the larger American purpose was a more effective detente with Moscow. Another was to convince the Maoist government and its successors that their cooperation with Washington would not worsen and indeed would improve China's political, military and economic situation. A third was to overcome the biggest obstruction to improved relations with Peking—the Republic of China on Taiwan—in a manner not destructive of our Asian allies' confidence in American reliability.

The Shanghai Communique issued at the close of President Nixon's visit to China (February 27, 1972) embodied the hopes, compromises and ambiguities of the American-Chinese experiment. A similarity but not identity of strategic views emerges from the Communique. An expression of opposition to "hegemony," the Chinese euphemism for Soviet domination, was accepted reluctantly by the American side, then engaged in negotiating a SALT agreement with Moscow; the United States more willingly opposed "great power rivalry" in South Asia. The practical side of such opposition—a working political and military alliance—did not emerge. As for the Republic of China on Taiwan, the United States and the PRC agreed to disagree. Still, the Communique gives evidence of the direction of U.S. policy: Washington did not challenge the contention (held by both the Communists and the Nationalists) that there is only one China and Taiwan is part of it. The United States reaffirmed its interests in a peaceful settlement of the Taiwan question. The ultimate American objective was the withdrawal of U.S. forces from Taiwan; they would be reduced gradually "as tension in the area diminishes."

The policy enunciated by Washington in the Communique began the process of reconciling U.S.-PRC strategic and regional views, a process now taken much further by President Carter. Carter, in recognizing Peking, reaffirmed that "hegemony" should be opposed in the Asian-Pacific region and anywhere else. He also removed a great symbolic barrier by derecognizing the Republic of China on Taiwan. These actions suggested that the strategic and regional reasons for rapprochement with Peking remain as strong as ever; they also implied that the strategic views of the two governments were rapidly approaching each other. But such pronouncements give little indication of their practical consequences. Important questions must be answered: How important is the "China card" to the U.S.-USSR strategic balance? How influential is U.S.-PRC collaboration in "stabilizing" Asian affairs? How will U.S.-USSR relations be affected? Will this contribute to more or less tension? What is the impact of derecognition on American allies? How will Taiwan's fate influence the success or failure of American policy?

The New Strategic Relationship

The strategic benefits of associating the United States and the PRC appear to be both obvious and substantial. A tacit alliance between Washington and Peking strengthens the "second front" facing Moscow. A reduction of Soviet capability to threaten Western Europe, to operate in Asia and Africa, and to upset the U.S.-USSR military balance, would seem to be a corollary. Carter's moves to bolster relations in the PRC thus appear to convey a willingness to defend American global interests without unnecessary risk.

In reality, however, the immediate dangers posed to the Russians by the new U.S.-PRC connection are not very great.

Let us assess the China card in its crudest form: military power. China has the largest military force in the world in terms of manpower, but China's military position cannot be gauged solely by this measure. Of all the countries of the world, China shares the longest border in the world with a hostile nation: the Soviet Union. China, in fact, has hostile nations on other borders: India and Vietnam. Peking's resources are limited. Military spending is far less than that of the Soviet Union and the United States—estimated in recent years at about 20-25 per cent of U.S. defense spending. [1]

At issue is whether a tacit U.S.-PRC alliance can compensate for present weakness. Chinese forces, like the Chinese economy, cannot be modernized overnight. Hence, new U.S. ties with China cannot quickly reverse even the PRC's military inferiority to Soviet forces on its borders, much less alter the U.S.-USSR balance of power. [2]

An examination of the PRC's military establishment reveals serious limitations not likely to be overcome without considerable foreign assistance. Chinese nuclear-weapons capabilities are severely limited in number, range and survivability. Chinese delivery systems fall short of the requirements of a credible deterrent against Soviet attack. Approximately forty IRBMs and a like number of MRBMs are the principal elements of the PRC's deterrent force. But this small force of missiles, liquid-fueled and unprotected by hardened silos, is vulnerable to a disarming first strike. China's eighty TU-16 intermediate-range bombers likewise are not a force capable of threatening Moscow or Leningrad.

Other Chinese weapons exhibit serious weaknesses. Many of the aircraft used by the Chinese Air Force are obsolete MIG 17s and 19s. China has built its own jet fighter plane, the F-9, but production slowed on this plane several years ago. Finally, Chinese planes lack all weather capabilities, air-to-air missiles and missile-avoidance equipment. In terms of quality the Chinese Air Force is below India's.

Similar problems confront the Chinese Navy. It has

fewer destroyers than Japan, France or Italy, and no aircraft carriers—which the Indian and Australian navies both possess. It also conspicuously lacks amphibious capabilities. Its strength is in submarines, but they are all older craft that move slowly and are easily detected.

China's present military value to the United States, then, appears to be primarily a passive one: tying down Soviet forces on the Sino-Soviet border. U.S. Defense Secretary Harold Brown noted that the Soviets have stationed "as much as a quarter of their ground on tactical air forces in the vicinity of China." As seen from Moscow, however, China's formidable standing army of 3 million to 6 million men makes it a grave potential menace if it is supplied with modern arms.

In addition to Soviet forces deployed along the Chinese border, we must examine the ever-increasing Soviet naval activities in the Pacific. That Soviet naval activities are global in nature was demonstrated by the Okean II exercise held in April 1975. In these exercises, personally commanded by the Soviet Naval Commander-in-Chief, Admiral Sergei Gorshkov, massive Soviet naval task forces were deployed simultaneously in the North and South Atlantic, the Mediterranean, the Indian Ocean and in the Sea of Japan. [3]

In the Okean II exercise, four Soviet naval task forces were deployed around Japan. One task force was identified in the Sea of Japan, another maneuvered around the Sea of Okhotsk north of Hokkaido, a third was spotted around 200 miles to the east of Japan, while a fourth was identified cruising between the Caroline Islands and the Philippines.

The Soviet Pacific Fleet is now larger than the U.S. Seventh Fleet. The number and quality of the Soviet naval vessels, ranging from Vladivostok to the Strait of Malacca and on to the Gulf of Aden's incipient basing system help to project Soviet influence around Asia. With the November 1978 signing of the Soviet-Vietnam Friendship Treaty the Soviets probably obtained operational use of the American-built Naval Base at Camranh Bay for its Pacific fleet. There is some evidence that the Kiev carrier will be deployed from Camranh Bay to operate in the South China Sea. Peking is worried that this development may open the way for Soviet naval dominance in the Western Pacific. [4] This development also makes Taiwan—the connecting chain link between Northeast and Southeast Asia—all the more important strategically.

Peking's leaders are obviously aware of the deficiencies of their armed forces in contrast to those of the Soviet Union both on land and at sea. As Vice Premier Teng told Hedley Donovan just prior to making his visit to Washington: "If we really want to be able to place curbs on the polar bear, the only realistic thing for us is to unite. If we only depend on the strength of the U.S., it is not enough. If we only depend on the strength of Europe, it is not enough. We are an insignificant, poor country, but if we unite, well, it will then carry weight." [5]

The Soviet Union's reaction has also taken these elements into account. The Soviets quickly answered the U.S.-China link-up with their own strategic moves: the formation of a possible "second front" to China by backing the Vietnamese attack on Cambodia, and the build up of Soviet garrisons on two islands close to Northern Hokkaido, claimed by the Japanese. This was done to apply coercive, diplomatic pressure on Japan for moving closer to China.

More significantly, the Soviets have begun to define their "tolerance" of a U.S.-PRC relationship and, indeed, of the entire Western alliance's connection to Peking. Moscow has suggested already the limitations it hopes to fasten on Washington's policy. On November 12, 1978, the influential Georgi Arbatov, head of the Kremlin's "think tank" on U.S.-Soviet relations (The Institute for the Study of the U.S.A. and Canada) expressed his concern over the formation of an incipient anti-Soviet alliance comprising the United States, Japan, the PRC and NATO. He discussed a number of possibilities, including the following: "One—which I hope will not materialize—is for China to become some sort of military ally to the West, even an informal ally. Then the whole situation would look different to us. We would have to re-analyze our relationship with the west." [6]

The Carter Administration's attempt to reassure the Soviets, however, produced a misunderstanding when the President's description of a Brezhnev message on the China card as "very positive in tone" was contradicted by Moscow. Later, after Chinese Deputy Prime Minister Teng Hsiao-ping denounced the Soviet Union as a threat to world peace during his official visit to the United States, Soviet Prime Minister Aleksei N. Kosygin complained to high-ranking Americans that this should have been "refuted" by the Carter Administration. [7] Diplomatic irritations aside, what troubles the Kremlin most is the PRC's determination to acquire modern arms from Japan, the United States and Western Europe.

Should the United States provide arms and military technology to China? The American government has committed itself to a "balanced" relationship with the Soviet Union and China, suggesting that arms will be sold to the PRC only if they are also offered to the Soviet Union. Any explicit military "tilt" towards the PRC would endanger the continuing SALT process with the Soviet Union—at the least. In effect, the Soviet leaders argue that China is not a major strategic military power and American attempts to make it one will strain detente beyond all credibility. It is also questionable whether Sino-American military cooperation would succeed in giving China a credible deterrent against the Soviet Union. Certainly for some years it would not. And if it did, would this be in the U.S. interests?

It seems unlikely that the Soviet Union will do nothing to prevent the rapid modernizing and arming of the PRC. We must also be aware that the chief card in the Kremlin's hand is a military one, a condition reinforced by the diplomatic situation in the Far East where the Soviets have lost ground with Japan and the Brezhnev "collective security" scheme has found few takers. Consequently, Soviet perceptions of the implication of President Carter's recognition of Peking might produce heightened tensions. There are many areas where the Soviets could harass or damage the PRC and an attack on an important Chinese border province should not be ruled out. The odds against the PRC in any such confrontation are formidable. Soviet ground forces in Asia comprise 44-45 divisions in an arc around Manchuria.

Thus, Carter's recognition of China, rather than marking a new era of international calm, may be a milestone on the road to international conflict. If in the short run, the new U.S.-PRC association cannot shift the world balance of power in our favor, we will have succeeded only in antagonizing the Soviet Union at a time when we may not be prepared to deal with the consequences.

Regional Stability in Asia

The U.S. recognition of Peking leaves the strategic future subject to several imponderables: Western participation in the PRC's military modernization, the deterrence in Moscow that this may produce and, conversely, whatever actions, diplomatic or military, Moscow can take to prevent the PRC's emergence as a superpower. The act of normalization thus begins another chapter in a strategic story as yet untold. A more certain conclusion, however, can be determined on the issue of regional stability.

The equilibrium in Asia is a highly dynamic one: the changes introduced by the U.S. tie with Peking have released forces which, historically, have given rise to international conflict. The United States, after withdrawing from Vietnam, reduced its ground forces in South Korea and in the long run hopes to leave entirely. During the same period, the Soviet Union continued to enlarge its forces in many areas of East Asia. American actions have done little to reassure nervous friends and allies that Washington can be counted upon in a military crisis. It is against this background that the act of normalization should be seen, for it raised anew the fate of Taiwan, an island with a crucial geopolitical significance.

Taiwan is the connecting link between U.S. security arrangements in Northeast and Southeast Asia. The United States has bilateral defense treaties with Japan, South Korea and the Philippines. The United States is also a signatory to the Manila Pact involving U.S. ties with both the Philippines and Thailand. An hour's flight from Clark field and Okinawa, Taiwan is part of the defensive perimeter of Japan and South Korea.

U.S. military access to Taiwan has been supportive of all U.S. deployments in the Western Pacific. Its several harbors can berth the entire U.S. Seventh Fleet; its many air bases can handle any aircraft in the world. The island also offers intelligence facilities to monitor Soviet naval activities in the Far East.

The U.S. decision to terminate the U.S.-ROC Defense Pact has created a number of serious uncertainties. ROC leaders may perceive that the only way they can retain their independence is to proclaim it, thereby challenging Peking to try to "liberate" Taiwan. Taiwan could also seek closer relations with the Soviet Union in three possible scenarios: 1) an understanding that if the PRC builds up forces in Fukien Province adjacent to Taiwan in preparation for an invasion, the Kremlin will increase tension on the Sino-Soviet border; 2) allowing the Soviet Navy and Air Force the use of bases in Taiwan; 3) signing a formal alliance with the Soviet Union.

Possible Soviet acquisition of Taiwanese ports of Keelung and Kaohsiung would complete the encirclement of China starting from Vladivostok and Soviet-aligned Vietnam to the south and Mongolia to the north. [8] At the same time, the Soviets would have no desire to see a hostile China acquire major bases in Taiwan that would enable Peking to dominate the Taiwan Strait, and extend its power into the Western Pacific. [9] In addition, Moscow's "Taiwan card" seems more plausible after the full diplomatic normalization between Washington and Peking.

Taiwan's third option is to build nuclear weapons. ROC scientists have been doing research on nuclear energy since the 1950s. The ROC has signed the Nuclear Nonproliferation Treaty and has made other promises not to build nuclear weapons. Nonetheless, there is reason to believe that Taiwan can and might do so as circumstances change. (These three options are discussed in a subsequent chapter in greater detail.)

If U.S. moves result in Taipei negotiating with Peking on the latter's terms and the eventual incorporation of Taiwan by the PRC, both the Soviet Union and Japan, not to mention South Korea and many nations of Southeast Asia, would feel threatened. Once part of China, Taiwan would give Peking control over the Taiwan Strait and thus the ability to challenge both the Soviet Navy and Japanese shipping in the area. Both Russia and Japan wish Taiwan to remain out of the PRC's hands and may perceive a serious threat if the island is incorporated into China. On the other hand, the United States, Japan, and the PRC would be greatly concerned were the Soviet Union to establish military liaison with Taiwan.

A quick survey of other critical U.S. relationships in the area will demonstrate how derecognition of Taiwan and its ambiguous future unsettle rather than stabilize the present situation in Asia.

In the Korean peninsula, tension has hardly abated a quarter century after the end of the Korean war. The government of South Korea again sought a rapprochement with North Korea shortly after the United States completed the process of normalization with the PRC. Ideological and economic differences, not to mention mutual hatred, make the outcome of the overtures problematic.

At present the North Korean government is still awaiting an opportunity to attack and defeat the South. North Korea has fielded a formidable fighting force superior to South Korea's in every area of *ready* military power. The North Korean forces are poised to attack without warning, and can move independently of both Moscow and Peking. In his FY 1980 report, Secretary of Defense Brown expressed his concern about "the possibility of a surprise attack by North Korea." [10]

A Sino-American alliance could prompt North Korea to tilt toward the Soviet Union and obtain Soviet support for a stepped up military pressure on South Korea or even an offensive. Alternatively, an alliance between North Korea and the Soviet Union to China's exclusion could precipitate more serious Sino-Soviet differences and even an outbreak of hostility between the PRC and the USSR. Likewise, South Korea may perceive that it is being abandoned by the United States and threaten to initiate hostilities to revitalize the American commitment.

One result of the Peking recognition has been to nudge North Korea closer to Moscow than Peking. Like most other small countries the Democratic People's Republic of Korea (DPRK) seeks to avoid total dependence on any single external power; and its strategy is to play off the Russians and Chinese when it is feasible. But on New Year's Eve, 1979, a Soviet-North Korean transportation protocol was reportedly signed in Moscow. Accordingly, the Soviet merchant marine will have substantially increased usage of the strategically located Najin Port on North Korea's east coast. [11] The port is located within fifty miles of the Korean-Soviet border in the Sea of Japan. In an apparent move against Peking, the Soviet Union is thought to want naval bases at the ports of Nampo and Haeju on the west coast of North Korea opposite China, and is even thought to have its eye on possible facilities at the ports of Shinuiju and Yon-gampo, virtually on the Chinese border at the very mouth of the Yalu River. [12]

The normalization of Sino-U.S. relations has already introduced delicate nuances into U.S.-Japanese relations, particularly with respect to their mutual security arrangements. As one of the few global economic powers, Japan strives for a stable four-power equilibrium in the Pacific. In this regard, Tokyo would like, even after signing the friendship treaty with China in August 1978, to have better relations with Moscow.

The Japanese perceive that the Soviets want them to remain militarily weak and unattached to either the United States or China. The Soviets doubtless realize that Soviet-Japanese defense cooperation is unattainable. The Soviet design for an Asian collective security system is perceived by the

Japanese as an attempt at facilitating the establishment of Soviet hegemony in Asia and to contain China. [13]

Although Chinese leaders have recently expressed support for Japan's defense pact with the United States and even its rearming, it must be remembered that Peking has long feared Japan's rearmament and only recently has spoken of renewed Japanese "militarism." In fact, after the Shanghai Communique was signed, Chinese leaders gave special assurances to North Korea of their support against Japan. If the United States were to give or facilitate military assistance to the PRC, the consequence might be either to 1) undermine the U.S.-Japan Security Treaty by eroding the Japanese belief that it is the main U.S. partner in Asia or 2) induce Japan to rearm, damaging U.S. relations with other nations in Asia that fear a rearmed Japan even if done with U.S. approval. [14] (Indonesia is one such country.)

U.S. security guarantees to Japan have been losing credibility because of a series of major U.S. decisions made without consulting Japan (for example, the opening to China, the Nixon "shocks" of 1971 and the perfunctory consultation on Korean withdrawals), and in the context of U.S.-Japan trade difficulties. Many Japanese fear that the United States will use its political influence to compete unfairly with Japan in the China market.

Japan and China have been historical competitors in Asia. Moreover, there is a territorial dispute lingering between the two countries that might one day bring them into confrontation. This concerns the potentially great oil deposits in the East China Sea which is claimed by both of them and South Korea. Thus, if the United States continues to base its Asian strategy upon its alliance with Japan, and simply assumes that it can ally with both Japan and China against the Soviet Union, a close relationship with the PRC, especially one involving assistance to a Chinese military buildup, may undermine the U.S.-Japanese association. Historically the United States has never had close relations with both China and Japan at the same time.

There is also a deep concern in Japan regarding the status of U.S. military commitments to South Korea and Taiwan. In the U.S.-Japanese Security Treaty, Taiwan is included in that treaty's definition of the Far East. Taiwan has long been recognized as a part of the Japanese security perimeter and remains so regardless of changes in its diplomatic status. At the close of 1978, Japanese Foreign Minister Sunao Sonoda, responding to a question in the Diet, recognized with alarm the possibility of the Soviet Union gaining influence in the Taiwan Strait after termination of the U.S.-Taiwan mutual defense treaty. [15]

Until recently a small Japanese defense establishment has been acceptable to both the United States and Japan. Recent events are forcing an agonizing Japanese reappraisal. These include: the growth of Soviet power and the associated Soviet coercive diplomacy toward Japan; the U.S. pullout decision with respect to Korea and Taiwan; concern over the relative weight the United States assigns to China and Japan; the absence of a U.S.-Japan concept for the future role of Japan in Asian security; and growing consideration in Japan of alternatives that would be inimical to U.S. interests in Asia.

Finally, the U.S.-PRC connection has been challenged in a spectacular fashion by the Vietnamese invasion of Cambodia. This act, encouraged by Soviet arms and a Friendship Treaty between Hanoi and Moscow, came only a month after President Carter's recognition of Peking. The Cambodians still resisting the Vietnamese army are being aided by the Chinese. The PRC, after massing large forces along the border with Vietnam, attacked its neighbor in keeping with Vice Premier Teng's declaration that Vietnam must be "punished." The United States has tried to put some distance between itself and this dangerous confrontation by condemning the Vietnamese invasion and warning the Chinese against war. Even if the Chinese withdraw their forces from Vietnam, the heightened tensions this action will introduce in Sino-Soviet relations cannot be erased. Under these circumstances it may not be enough to state that "We are not taking sides in the struggle between Communist states in Asia." [16]

Thailand, whose independence is crucial to ASEAN, is particularly vulnerable to Vietnam pressure if Hanoi consolidates control over all of Indochina. President Carter assured the Thai Prime Minister, Kriangsak Chamanan, that the United States would take "definite action if the fighting in Cambodia threatened Thai security." [17] Consequently, developments in Southeast Asia could place the United States in an extremely awkward situation with its credibility as a major power in the balance.

The Future of U.S. China Policy

The strategic and regional aspects of Washington's decision to recognize Peking reveal a complex mosaic of a shifting power balance, mixed motivations and dangerously ambiguous expectations. Taken at its broadest, U.S. policy in East Asia over the last decade has sought to achieve a four-legged balance of power: the United States, Japan, China and the Soviet Union. Inasmuch as the Soviet Union is the expanding power and at least the dominant threat to the other three it is the focus of a tacit alliance among the United States, Japan, and China. This process of alliance, at the center of which is the U.S.-PRC rapprochement, remains problematical.

First, the effort to create a new balance of power may not succeed because the nations involved do not possess similar aims, arms or influence. Only the United States and the Soviet Union are superpowers. The injection of the PRC into these power calculations suggests a measure of military might that the PRC does not possess. The balance, in any case, is a complex one, and may be altered by other factors.

Second, a purpose behind the normalization effort appears to be to enhance stability in East Asia—an area of the world where America holds strong economic interests and faces major dangers. The Korean Peninsula is tense with old antagonism and new arms. In Southeast Asia, the scene of domineering Vietnamese armies, we have renewed our pledge to support Thailand, a signatory of the Manila Pact. Taiwan is a nation to which the

American people remain committed. We also retain bilateral alliances with a number of Asian countries and are still bound by ANZUS and other defense systems. In this environment, stability may be elusive indeed.

A third factor already mentioned is the traditional rivalry of China and Japan. It remains to be seen whether a long-term alliance between China and Japan can be developed. There are a number of issues, such as Korea or Taiwan or off-shore oil that could become sources of enmity in Sino-Japanese relations.

Fourth, U.S. policy toward China has been greatly influenced by the Sino-Soviet dispute. In the past Washington has remained friendlier with both Moscow and Peking than they are with each other. But should one side or the other conclude that its basic interests were being jeopardized by the trend of U.S. policy, then preventive action—diplomatic and military—might be precipitated.

An imbalance in American diplomacy toward one party in the Sino-Soviet dispute could have a particularly unfortunate impact in Southeast Asia. The United States needs to remain involved in Southeast Asia and should play a major role in moderating, controlling or balancing Sino-Soviet differences.

The subtleties of playing the China card thus involve a number of factors, including China's military capabilities, the extent of the PRC's expectations with regard to the continuing American role in East Asia, possible moves by the Soviet Union to establish new ties with Taiwan and to wean North Korea from Peking, and apparent American desires to reduce military responsibilities in Northeast Asia. Any one of those factors could disrupt the strategic calculations of the normalization decision, and undermine any advantage gained by the switch of diplomatic recognition from the ROC to the PRC. Unfortunately, the future of each factor may also be in large part beyond the control of the current American administration; playing a diplomatic card has only short-term advantages unless the act is part of a meaningful, long-term strategy. But the Carter Administration has not made clear the name of the larger game. Indeed, the rationale for normalization may be rooted in contradictory expectations: the PRC expecting the United States to do more against Soviet influence, the United States expecting the PRC to do more, and neither able to do enough.

If anything, our new ties with China have increased the chances of a major Sino-Soviet eruption. In these circumstances the military use of Taiwan by either China or Russia would be regarded as a hostile act by the other. For this reason the future security of an independent Taiwan is more important now than before Carter recognized Peking and introduced new uncertainties into the security equation of East Asia.

Thus, some kind of U.S.-Taiwan defense commitment remains essential if the island is to avoid capture by the PRC, co-option by the Soviet Union, or a decision to produce nuclear weapons, any one of which might precipitate strategic or regional consequences our policy is designed to avoid. A U.S. commitment to a secure Taiwan is essential if the strategic and regional benefits of closer U.S.-PRC relations are to be realized. Meanwhile, the immediate future promises tests for the new U.S.-PRC partnership—perhaps at times and places of the Soviets' own choosing.

Chapter Two
THE ECONOMIC BASIS OF
U.S. CHINA POLICY

Although economic considerations seemingly played a minor role in President Carter's decision to recognize Peking, they have subsequently been advanced as a major benefit from this action. Secretary of the Treasury W. Michael Blumenthal predicted on December 20, 1978 that as "normalization" proceeds between the United States and the People's Republic of China, "the growth in trade will be fairly rapid." Blumenthal also informed reporters that he will make a trip to China early next year "as the senior Cabinet member on economic affairs," and that his mission will be to set up a broad framework for expanded economic relationships. [1] In addition to Blumenthal, Christopher Phillips, President of the National Council for U.S.-China Trade, believes that if the claims and the most-favored-nation (MFN) issues are settled, there are no upper limits to the U.S.-China trade possibilities. [2]

The case for recognition or non-recognition of Peking has also been couched in economic terms in the past. For their part, the leaders of the PRC perceive commercial profit as the motive force in capitalist nations' foreign policies; they do not view the United States as an exception. In fact, it is precisely for this reason that they have often made their appeal to the United States for full recognition in economic terms and have clearly used the "vast China market" as bait to Americans. Both before and since recognition the Carter Administration has sought support for its China policy from American companies and businessmen that are doing business with China. Still, there are important obstacles to the establishment of full trade relations between the United States and the PRC. The first is the question of claims by private U.S. citizens whose assets were seized in 1949 or before. The second major roadblock to normalization is the absence of most-favored-nation treatment for China's exports to this country. Because Chinese exports, like those of most other communist states, do not enjoy MFN treatment, tariffs on their goods shipped here are up to 300 per cent higher than for nations accorded MFN treatment.

American businessmen will be expected to support, if not to help to attain, U.S. goals in Asia. We therefore need to examine U.S.-China policy in the context of the economic and commercial issues. In this context, one must ask: What are the gains to be obtained from recognizing Peking, and what will be lost by breaking formal ties with Taipei? What are the economic advantages and liabilities of diplomatic ties with either? How will this influence our trade with other countries and our reputation? What are the future possibilities and the likely dangers involved in dealing economically with Peking or Taiwan? Is it possible to deal commercially with both? Now that we have recognized Peking, what provisions should we make to preserve what we have done for Taiwan economically as well as our current investment there? What are the attitudes of the two Chinas in reference to this question?

To begin with, we must examine America's past, as well as present, involvement in the economy of Taiwan. The change in America's stance toward the PRC will probably entail sacrificing some business ties with Taiwan. This must be seen against uncertain gains in the case of commercial ties with China. It is necessary to look at what we will be giving up. The initial motive behind American aid to Taiwan was to fight the spread of Communism; consequently most aid took the form of military assistance. Other aid was made available to stabilize the economy, i.e., to provide basic goods that were in short supply.

Although the major portion of U.S. aid given to Taiwan in ensuing years continued to be defined as military aid, by 1954-1955 more and more funds were channeled into development projects. In 1958 the U.S. Congress created the Development Loan Fund, and in 1959 the Industrial Development and Investment Center and the China Development Corporation were set up in Taipei to use American aid more efficiently and to foster economic development. [3] Subsequently, U.S. aid officials proposed a comprehensive plan to the ROC government to help direct funds into private investment and expand exports; the next year, Taipei responded and passed the nineteen-point Program of Economic and Financial Reform. Taiwan thus became an experimental ground for U.S. aid in Asia, and in the eyes of one expert "virtually every idea and formula invented was tried." [4] Taiwan also became the recipient of more American aid on a per capita basis than any other nation at peace.

The impact of American aid was as impressive as its breadth and depth. By the late 1950s Taiwan was on the way to sustained economic growth, and in 1960 Washington advised Taipei to anticipate the early end of U.S. economic help. Following American advice Taipei began to expand its exports to compensate for the loss of U.S. financial assistance, which had served as a primary source of foreign exchange. Thus when U.S. aid ended in 1965, Taiwan was prepared and the adjustment was smooth. In short, U.S. aid to Taiwan was a tremendous success story for the U.S. economic assistance program. Taiwan was one of the few developing countries to attain rapid, sustained growth after a short period of U.S. aid.

Owing to the importance of its aid, as well as to the ROC's dependence on Washington for military and political support, the United States attained a great deal of influence in Taiwan in the areas of planning and modernization. The economic and financial reform of 1960 made possible the more efficient use of aid funds. American influence also extended into such areas as land reform, and eventually into almost every facet of economic development, and to a considerable extent into politics. In the words of one observer: "American technicians were involved in almost every major social institution, public and private." [5]

Land reform in Taiwan, because of its success, became a model and therefore deserving of special attention. In part the product of the Nationalists' bitter lesson in China and their determination to govern the rural sector properly, as well as the fortunate situation of owing nothing to Taiwanese landlords and having land formerly owned by the Japanese to distribute, Taiwan's land reform program was a success. However, effective land use was also a result of U.S. influence and advice. [6] Revolution in the use of farm land occurred in three steps. First, rent was reduced 37.5 per cent and landlords were forced to sign leases for a minimum of six years. Second, formerly Japanese-owned or occupied land was sold to the farmers in order to make them "capitalist" owners. Third, the Land to the Tiller Act was passed, forcing large-scale landlords to sell their lands to the government, which were in turn sold to the peasants. Thus, in contrast to 1948 when only 55 per cent of the land was owned by cultivators, by 1959 it was over 85 per cent. [7] In terms of productivity, as measured by agricultural export earnings, the results were little short of fantastic: export earnings increased from $7 million to $40 million for raw agricultural products during the five-year period 1950-1955, and from $63 million in 1951 to $125 million in 1957 for processed products. [8] In contrast, the PRC also undertook a land reform program which resulted, according to conservative estimates, in the killing of 2 million landlords and rich peasants. It also engendered food shortages, eventually causing the national level of health to decline and thousands to flee into Hong Kong and elsewhere. [9]

The U.S.-inspired land reform and rural reconstruction programs in Taiwan had a number of beneficial side effects. Rural income increased, fostering considerably more equality in income and more even distribution of wealth. Higher incomes on the farms also made possible higher education for rural children and a marked rise in the standards of health and welfare in Taiwan. The government program to buy land as part of the "Land to the Tiller" program also forced private investment in the industrial sector, thus promoting the growth of small industry which provided employment opportunities in the cities and increased the rate of urbanization.

U.S. aid to build infrastructure projects, together with funds that were forced into the private sector of the economy further fostered a capitalist form of economic development, but one which because of the emphasis on smaller business, together with the fact that the business sector was dominated by the less-well-off Taiwanese, helped promote further income leveling. Meanwhile the United States favored more specialization in industry and products that could be exported. From 1952 to 1968, Taiwan's exports increased from $111 million to $842 million, or a compound growth rate of 11.1 per cent. [10] This had the effect of providing foreign exchange so that Taiwan could eventually be weaned from U.S. aid while at the same time tying its economy to the international market place. Parallel to these developments, Taiwan's economic stability and export orientation provided opportunities for foreign investment in Taiwan by Americans, Japanese and Overseas Chinese businessmen.

The annual increase in GNP jumped quickly: from 3.7 per cent in 1957 to 9.6 per cent during the period 1960 to 1965. [11] And in spite of rapid population increases and a high rate of per capita investment, income and buying power rose almost as fast as economic growth rates. Thus by the 1960s, with United States help, encouragement and advice, Taiwan had created a successful, growing consumer-capitalist economy oriented toward international trade.

The United States, however, did not simply help Taiwan's economic growth and then let it fend for itself. After 1965, when U.S. aid ceased, Washington gave Taiwan access to the U.S. market and encouraged United States businessmen to invest in Taiwan. This stimulated the economy even more than aid and made possible even higher rates of economic growth: from 1965 to 1972 GNP increased at an average annual rate of over 10 per cent. [12] And because of the importance of the United States market, together with U.S. investment, military sales and political support, Washington maintained a considerable degree of influence over Taiwan both economically and politically, even after aid was ended.

Because of economic growth both the standard and the style of living in Taiwan changed markedly. The magnitude of this can only be demonstrated by citing some relevant figures. In 1952 the average yearly income in Taiwan was $148; in 1977 it was $1,079. During this same period the average life span increased from 58 to 71 years. The percentage of households with electricity increased from just over 35 per cent to 99 per cent; the number of households with T.V. sets increased from zero to over 95 per cent. [13] The number of radios increased thirteenfold from 1953 to 1962. The number of telephones increased more than 500 per cent in the decade after 1965. [14] At the present time most households have a refrigerator and a variety of other household appliances. Many have air-conditioners. Most families also have a motorcycle or car.

Rapid economic growth in Taiwan, moreover, was not accompanied by increasing income disparities. In fact, incomes leveled out and disparities or differentials in incomes diminished. Because of this, Taiwan should be regarded as an outstanding example and a model for developing countries to follow. The average difference in income in Taiwan—according to the Gini scale, a measure used by economists to measure income disparities—is less than in most European countries, the United States or Japan. [15]

Washington informed Taipei in 1960 that it would discontinue aid to the Republic of China by 1965. The ROC, heeding American advice, actively sought foreign investment to create export industries to compensate for the loss of U.S. aid. In 1960 the ROC government enacted the Statute for the Encouragement of Foreign Investment, which offered incentives to foreign businesses such as a five-year tax-free period, a 15 per cent tax limit on net gains thereafter, accelerated depreciation provisions, duty-free import privileges for materials used in the production of goods for export, and the repatriation of capital and profits. In 1965, the year that U.S. aid stopped, the ROC government wrote legislation establishing export-processing zones that extended free port privileges to foreign-owned companies that exported their products. Zones were subsequently established in Kaohsiung, Nantse and Taichung.

Encouraged by this legislation and the spirit of cooperation that accompanied it, as well as being aware of the fact that investment prospects in Western Europe were not as bright

26

in the 1960s as they had been earlier, American investors began to go to Taiwan in sizable numbers. By 1977 U.S. private investment in Taiwan (individuals and firms) had reached more than $300 million. In addition, U.S. banks and the Export-Import Bank had committed $1.5 billion to Taiwan. [16]

About one-half of U.S. investment in Taiwan has gone to finance the so-called "ten large projects"—infrastructure projects that include a shipyard, a steel mill, a petrochemical complex, nuclear power plants, a superhighway, electrified rail lines, ports and a new airport. Inasmuch as the economic feasibility of some of these projects was doubted at the onset both by American and Chinese experts, it appeared that Americans were putting their money into the projects because the U.S. government encouraged and guaranteed their investment. The ROC government undertook them in large part for political legitimacy. [17] This is a particularly salient point if one recalls the new emphasis given to the projects in 1972—the year after Taiwan was expelled from the United Nations, which was followed by the flight of embassies from Taipei to Peking. Thus, the United States seemed to be helping the ROC survive the challenge to its legitimacy by facilitating its continued rapid economic growth. [18]

By 1978 nearly two dozen United States banks had branches in Taiwan, in addition to the plants and offices of a large number of American companies, including RCA, Admiral, Sylvania, General Instrument, Zenith, Gulf Oil Company, E. I. Du Pont, Amoco, Cities Service, Goodrich, American Cyanamid, Union Carbide, General Motors, Ford, Pfizer, Lilly, ITT, Textron, IBM, General Electric, Corning Glass, Timex, Bulova, National Distillers, Singer, Scott Paper Company, Mattel and others. Clearly the pace of United States business involvement in Taiwan quickened even while the United States government was pursuing detente with Peking.

The same trends are visible in terms of U.S. trade with Taiwan. In the fiscal year 1963 total two-way U.S.-ROC trade amounted to $220 million, or 26.6 per cent of Taiwan's imports and 17.1 per cent of Taiwan's exports. Japan's trade with Taiwan was considerably more than United States trade—31.1 and 31.4 per cent respectively. [19] By 1966, however, the United States had replaced Japan as Taiwan's most important trading partner, and the upward trend continued. In 1971 U.S.-ROC total two-way trade was over $1.61 billion; in 1972 it was $1.91 billion; in 1973 it was $2.94 billion; in 1976 it was $4.8 billion. [20] By 1977 the United States was taking 40 per cent of Taiwan's exports. [21] Notably, America continued to underwrite Taiwan's rapid growth during a period when the United States sought closer ties with the People's Republic of China. To most observers this suggested America's intent to have ties with both—to have a two-Chinas or a one-China, one-Taiwan policy. Clearly it did not suggest that the United States would soon acknowledge Taiwan as being part of China in order to establish formal ties with Peking.

Taiwan's economy is a capitalist one (in contrast to 1952 when 57 per cent of industrial production was government-owned and operated) and its society highly consumer-oriented—Western style. [22] The gap between Taiwan and China in other areas, such as customs, social norms and values, has also grown in the last two or more decades in direct proportion to economic growth—and to U.S. aid, investment and trade.

Possible Consequences of Taiwan's Incorporation

If Taiwan were eventually to become part of China, Peking would face the problem of ruling a province with a different kind of economy, standard of living, and an alien culture. Peking has created an essentially self-reliant economy—and the ROC has founded its prosperity on export-oriented growth. Harmonization of the issues of public and private ownership of land and businesses would create profound political tension. Finally, the disparity in consumer wealth between the people of the ROC and the PRC would induce conflict over the redistribution of wealth.

The direct financial losses to the United States by the

incorporation of "Taiwan province" into the PRC would be considerable. American investment would be lost for the most part. [23] American investors cannot expect to recover very much if Peking assumes real jurisdiction over Taiwan. The extensive trade between the United States and Taiwan could not be continued, and America's eighth ranking trading partner and a market for large quantities of American products, over $600 million in agricultural products alone in 1978, would be sacrificed. Special negotiations with Peking may help; but the Carter Administration, by agreeing that Taiwan is a part of China, gives investors very little legal recourse. Nor can American companies maintain trade ties at their present level. In short, abandoning Taiwan will be expensive for the United States.

Besides the direct losses to the United States, Washington also has to consider that Japan is a major investor in Taiwan and that its investment, being in smaller businesses and less liquid assets, would be even more difficult to recover than American investment. The same is true of Overseas Chinese investment in Taiwan. Both have depended upon the U.S. presence in Taiwan to protect their investments. Hence, if recognizing Peking leads to the complete abandoning of Taiwan, Washington will draw upon itself the resentments of some Japanese and Overseas Chinese businessmen, affecting United States commercial relations with Tokyo and a number of Southeast Asian countries.

U.S. Economic Prospects with the PRC

In order to assess the economic consequences of a pro-Peking China policy, it is now necessary to look at the scope of the U.S.-Chinese economic ties. More important, however, inasmuch as American economic ties with the PRC have been admittedly small, is the question of future potential for a PRC market for American goods. We should also direct our attention to specific questions such as the opportunities for United States investors in China, joint ventures, the commodities traded or that might be traded; whether there are any important strategic materials that the United States can purchase; and whether the United States might be able to sell surplus products to China. How increasing U.S.-PRC trade will affect other American trading partners is likewise an important question. We must also ask some questions concerning political preconditions to trade.

In terms of its size, as measured in gross national product, the Chinese economy is sixth largest in the world—after the United States, the Soviet Union, Japan, West Germany and France. However, China's GNP is only about one-half of Japan's, one-fourth of the European Economic Community's and one-fifth of the United States'. In relation to the world economy China contributes 4.7 per cent of the total global product. [24] In short, while China is a ranking economic power, its economic size does not compare to the world's economic giants, nor does China's economic status correspond to its population size (which makes it the largest nation in the world and between 20 and 25 per cent of the world's total population). The Chinese economy has been growing at a rate about equal to the global average, but much slower than Taiwan.

Foreign investment in China is essentially non-existent. China's exports have never exceeded 2 per cent of the world's total, while its total trade is only 5 to 6 per cent of its GNP—the lowest of any nation in Asia and the lowest of any major nation. [25] In terms of trade per capita China has only around $14 per year—near the bottom of all nations in the world. Moreover, foreign trade as a percentage of GNP has declined over the last two decades. In contrast, Taiwan's foreign trade as a percentage of GNP in 1977 was 78 per cent. United States-PRC trade totalled $326 million while United States-Taiwan trade was $5.5 billion or seventeen times the amount traded with China. [26]

Since Mao's death, China has increased its foreign borrowings (called deferred payments) and has increased its foreign trade considerably. And this trade has been mostly with the developed, capitalist countries. Thus, some Americans have become very hopeful about the possibilities of a major expansion in sales to China. There is a basic complementariness between the United States and the PRC's economy; this seems to present

United States businessmen with tangible opportunities. Trade possibilities between the United States and the PRC, however, must be assessed in greater depth to compare the economic consequences of choosing between Peking and Taipei.

It should be remembered that throughout United States history, trade with China has been a chimera. American trade with China has never constituted more than 2 per cent of total United States trade, and China has never been an important U.S. trading partner. [27] This was true despite Washington's historic emphasis upon keeping China "open" for trade; it remained the case even after the United States developed close political and therefore commercial relations with China in the 1930s and 1940s. During the latter period the United States share of the China trade varied between 15 and 19 per cent. If the United States could regain a comparable share in the China trade—which even the most optimistic have not suggested—United States-China trade would still be less than America's trade with Hong Kong or South Korea and only a fraction of U.S. trade with Taiwan. [28]

Although most experts predict that United States-China trade will increase, few believe that China will become a major trading partner. Throughout the last decade the PRC has been increasing its foreign trade by about 11-14 per cent per year in real terms—in contrast to the 1960s when Chinese foreign trade actually decreased. [29]

Assuming that Peking is able to increase this figure moderately in coming years, it will still have to restructure its trade with established partners in order to increase trade with the United States by any significant margin. Even if this is done there seems to be room for at most $1 billion to $2 billion in two-way trade in the 1980s—not a very important figure to the United States. [30]

On the more pessimistic side one must consider the fact that China may have already committed itself to the highest volume of trade feasible for the near future. A variety of reasons support this argument. First, China's sheer size makes for a large internal market. Transportation improvements in coming years will increase domestic trade and thus tend to reduce the need for foreign trade. At present much of China's international trade is economically feasible solely because of the cost and problems associated with domestic trade. Second, the PRC's economy is a planned one and central planners prefer domestic trade over international trade. It is unlikely that this will change significantly even in the context of China's current modernization campaign. There still may be opposition to increasing foreign trade because it makes China dependent upon foreign goods and inhibits the development of native industry. [31] Third, changes in the present leadership—which may occur soon, given the ages of some of the top leaders—may bring new policies which do not emphasize international commercial contacts as is the case now.

On the other hand, the importance of trade cannot be measured by trade volume alone. We must also ask the question: what will the United States sell to China, and what will China sell to the United States? Important Chinese exports of the past were tung oil, hog bristles and tin ore. Clearly none of these things are strategic to the United States; in fact, they are primarily things that the United States does or could produce itself or could import from a host of developing countries which endeavor to increase their share in the United States market. [32] China's export of metals has declined considerably in recent years and the most important export metals—manganese, tungsten, tin and mercury—are readily available on the world market in sufficient quantity to meet America's foreseeable needs. Petroleum is another possibility, but so far China is only the thirteenth largest producer of oil in the world with much less to export than its rank suggests because of domestic needs. Further, much of the oil produced in China has a high wax content and would be costly to refine. Most of the oil exports have already been promised to Japan. Even considering the possibility that China can increase its petroleum exports, it is unlikely much if any will go to the United States since the U.S. West Coast has an excess of oil from Alaska and the distance to the East Coast would make Chinese oil much more expensive.

Other items with export potential to the United States

are handicrafts and textiles. The market for the former is clearly inelastic and there is already evidence that it is a constricting market. Chinese artifacts became faddish after President Nixon's visit to China, but this has now faded. The textile market in the United States holds some promise since the United States' demand is so large; but this is problematic in that increased imports of textiles are sure to alienate American labor organizations as is already in evidence by union pressure on the federal government to set up quotas. [33] Inasmuch as the United States has been too generous in the eyes of U.S. labor—and as reflected in public opinion polls—in allowing developing countries into the United States market to sell textile products, there is little room to allow China even a meaningful part of that market.

The important products that Mainland China will import in the near future will be food, chemical fertilizer, machinery and equipment, copper and rubber. [34] China's imports of food are limited primarily to grains. In overall terms China is an exporter of food products; these constituted about one-fourth of Chinese exports by value in the 1950s and the 1960s. [35] China will no doubt continue to import wheat though production in China is increasing and may cause imports to decline somewhat. However, large purchases of U.S. grains will occur only in the case of intermittent crop failures. And China is not without other sources. To date it has purchased most of its wheat from Canada and Australia and may continue to do so in the future. In any event if the United States were to compete in this market, success could be attained only at the expense of two close allies. Chemical fertilizer machinery and equipment are important Chinese imports, but huge contracts have already been signed with Japan and several Western European countries; new purchases in this area are now declining. Copper and rubber are commodities that the United States cannot sell to China since the United States also imports these goods.

There is also significant potential for the United States to sell high-technology goods to China, such as computers and weapons. But political problems have arisen each time the United

States considered or allowed sales of such items to China, and opposition can be expected to arise in the future: from domestic sources, from our allies, and above all from the Soviet Union. [36] Washington must always consider the possibility of China using American technology or weapons against an Asian neighbor, especially one allied with the United States. The fact that Soviet weapons sold to China in the 1950s are now aimed at Russian cities is a vivid example of this dilemma.

The most serious limitations to increasing United States-China trade in the future then fall into four general categories: First, both countries are generally self-sufficient economies. Second, whereas China would like to import technology and technology-intensive goods and weapons from the United States, there are serious obstacles both in the United States and abroad. Third, China has little the United States needs to import and must compete with other developing countries already in the market. Fourth, China lacks foreign exchange to pay for U.S. imports and thus needs to sell more abroad; as noted earlier, Chinese export potential is seriously limited.

Inasmuch as China has regarded, and will no doubt continue to regard, its trade as a tool for obtaining political aims, it may be expected that Peking will make demands on the United States for access to the China market even though the trade advantages will clearly fall on the China side of the fence. Peking has already demonstrated this by buying more from the United States after the Shanghai Communique and then limiting trade when it perceived that the United States was not moving fast enough to fulfill the provisions of this agreement. [37]

There are a number of complications involved in United States economic relations with both Chinas, insofar as trade is tied both to recognition and to trade agreements and treaties. De-recognition of the ROC may cause problems for U.S. businessmen that might have been avoided by delaying this step until the proper legislation was written. Similarly, in terms of economic motives, Washington should have negotiated a number of economic issues with the PRC before granting diplomatic recognition. The White House should also have taken steps to have the

Congress nullify or write new laws to circumvent legislation that impedes U.S.-PRC trade.

One of the most difficult problems in expanding U.S.-PRC trade is the most-favored-nation provision in U.S. and international law. According to this provision, until January 1, 1979 the ROC was granted nondiscrimination rights in terms of the tariff applied to its goods imported into the United States. However, despite the granting of recognition to Peking, the MFN provision does not automatically transfer to the PRC. According to the American 1974 Trade Act, MFN cannot be extended to nations with whom the United States does not have bilateral trade agreements. If Taiwan is now "part" of China, MFN would be lost, unless an exception were made in American law. [38] Furthermore, according to the Jackson-Vanik Amendment of that act, MFN treatment is denied to nations that, among other things, block free emigration. The PRC would thus appear to be excluded from MFN. And if it were to be included, despite Jackson-Vanik, the same would have to be done for the Soviet Union if the appearance of "balanced" relations so eagerly sought by the Administration is to be sustained. [39]

Another important issue is the status of China for Export-Import Bank loans. According to its founding statute, the Bank is not allowed to deal with Communist countries. The President can make waivers to this provision, and has in the case of Yugoslavia, Romania, Poland and the Soviet Union. The President may not find it easy to obtain such a waiver for China if Congress remains irritated over his unilateral act of recognition, despite resolutions to the contrary. It bears repeating in this context that in June 1978 the Senate passed a resolution (94-0) telling the President he is to consult with the Senate before abrogating any treaty—with specific reference to the U.S.-ROC Mutual Defense Pact. The House subsequently adopted the resolution.

Another problem is that the Jackson-Vanik Amendment also applies to Export-Import Bank programs and thus affords another hindrance to allowing trade benefits to accrue to China or to American businessmen seeking commercial relations with China. Again, since President Carter acknowledged that Taiwan is part of China when recognizing the PRC, it would be assumed that Taiwan is legally part of China and thus subject to the same limitations. Alternatively Taiwan could be regarded as non-existent and contracts between the Bank and the ROC or American firms doing business in Taiwan would thereby be terminated. [40]

Operations of the Foreign Credit Insurance Corporation and the Overseas Private Investment Corporation are influenced in a similar way by the Export-Import Bank. Inasmuch as the former is an adjunct agency of the Export-Import Bank, the previous discussion applies. The functions of the FCIC and OPIC come under the heading of foreign aid, and so they can deal with neither a Communist country nor a country with which the United States has severed relations, and this is thus a double-edged sword in relation to current U.S. China policy. [41]

There are also a number of laws, regulations, and legal or customary provisions that present various difficulties concerning current American economic policies toward China. During the March 1979 visit to Peking by Secretary of the Treasury Michael Blumenthal, an agreement was signed to pay 41 cents on the dollar to American individuals and companies for the $196 million in assets seized by the PRC after 1949. Consequently the Johnson Debt Default Act no longer applies to U.S.-PRC economic relations. The People's Republic, however, does not allow foreign claimants to institute arbitration abroad—a widely practiced international custom of importance to American businessmen. A similar situation exists with patents, copyrights and trademarks: the PRC is not a member of the Paris Convention for the Protection of Industrial Property or the Universal Copyrights Convention. Thus such protections do not exist in the PRC. [42]

Problems for United States businessmen doing business with Taiwan in the context of current U.S. China policy are just as numerous. For example, can United States export regulations apply to Taiwan? Would citizens of Taiwan have access to United States courts to settle differences concerning agreements and contracts with American businessmen? The same question also applies to the rights of United States businessmen to use courts in Taiwan or other international organs in their disputes. Problems could also arise from United States anti-boycott laws in the event that Peking tries to squeeze Taiwan by pressuring United States businesses in China into not doing business with Taiwan.

Finally, some economic or commercial questions also have strong political ramifications. For instance, how long can the United States continue to sell weapons to Taiwan after normalization with the PRC? Can the United States continue to supply nuclear materials to Taiwan after derecognition? Will Washington have the right to demand controls over and the accountability of nuclear fuels already supplied to Taiwan? What about immigration from Taiwan? And what are the rights of ROC citizens to conduct business or even remain in the United States?

Weighing the Balances

The economic evidence indicates that the United States can gain little commercially from recognition of Peking. If arrangements can be worked out, Taiwan's volume of trade with the United States will still be larger than that of the PRC for at least the next decade. Peking faces major barriers to expansion of commercial exchange with the United States: a large debt and little to export as payment. The PRC is already buying all that it can from Europe and Japan and its buying will have to decrease in the next few years due to financing problems.

United States investment in Taiwan is large—over $5 hundred million—and it is a profitable investment. The potential to invest in the PRC is low and will doubtlessly remain so due to uncertainties over Chinese willingness to welcome substantial foreign investment.

The United States possessed considerable economic leverage with both the PRC and Taiwan: Taiwan depended upon the United States economy and the PRC sought access to the American market plus American technology and weapons. Washington could have easily pursued a two-Chinas policy. In fact the United States may still pursue such a policy even though it has already acknowledged that Taiwan is a part of China. In economic terms Taiwan and the PRC are two very separate entities and the United States can duel with both in spite of the problems already mentioned. It will be the strategy most acceptable to American businessmen. Any other policy would no doubt divide the business community and create bitterness among business and financial leaders, particularly those with investments in Taiwan.

In any event, the economic consequences of President Carter's act of "normalization" should be subordinated to the political requirements. Clearly it would be disadvantageous for the United States to accept any arrangement which forces the Taiwan economy either to go into isolation or to come under the authority of the central planners in Peking. Given the limited prospects for a massive increase in U.S. trade with the PRC, the ostensibly economic issues of devising new legislation for Taiwan and overcoming restrictions on most-favored-nation status for Peking, will be subject to strategic calculations. Above all, the problem of maintaining "equal treatment" for the Soviets will become evident as normalization confronts American laws governing international commerce.

Chapter Three
THE LEGAL DIMENSIONS OF U.S. CHINA POLICY

One of the major assumptions in U.S. foreign policy is that the United States supports international law to "create an orderly international system based on international law." [1] Thus, American relations with other nations must respect international legal standards; and solutions to problems should be handled in a legal context, or at least abide by global legal codes when applicable. Clearly, U.S. China policy should be no exception. President Carter, however, acknowledged that Taiwan is a part of China, and thereby reversed the gradual evolution of two Chinas, or one China and one Taiwan. He seemingly ignored a similar legal solution that has brought the two Germanies into a variety of international organizations and made possible diplomatic contacts with both. His action, however, did not resolve Taiwan's legal status and clearly does not transfer jurisdiction to the People's Republic of China.

Since 1949 there have been *de facto* two Chinas. The ROC, in terms of having diplomatic ties with a majority of the world's nations and having membership in the United Nations, until 1971, was the "legal" China. In October, Peking obtained the "China seat" at the United Nations, and since both governments insisted that only one Chinese state existed, Taipei was "expelled." A large portion of the nations that had formal ties with the ROC closed their embassies in Taipei and moved to Peking. Notwithstanding, most of the nations that left Taipei when they established relations with Peking only "took note" of Peking's claim to Taiwan, or said nothing about it at all. Few iterated Peking's stand that Taiwan is Chinese territory. Furthermore, the nations that broke relations with the ROC at this time were cognizant of an American military presence on Taiwan as well as diplomatic ties between the United States and the ROC. Thus they deferred the question.

In 1972, the United States signed a communique with Peking promising "normalization"—the Shanghai Communique. This document subsequently became the basis for the U.S.-PRC rapprochement as well as the foundation of U.S. China policy. The Shanghai Communique, however, is confusing when it says that "Chinese on either side of the Taiwan Strait agree that there is only one China." The word "either" may be taken to mean "each" in this case, though in proper English it would be more suggestive of one side and thus indicates no concurrence. The document, in also stating that the United States "does not challenge" the one China viewpoint, suggests nothing. [2] "Does not challenge" in the English version (the Chinese translation is different) suggests no position or opinion. What American diplomats seemed to be trying to do was improve relations with Peking and avoid the major problem by ambiguity.

Furthermore, in seeming contradiction to the spirit of the Shanghai Communique, President Nixon stated before he embarked on his trip to China that the "new dialogue would not be at the expense of old friends." [3] This obviously meant Taiwan. At almost the same time, Nixon asserted that the United States would maintain its friendship, diplomatic ties and defense commitment with the ROC. Henry Kissinger repeated Nixon's "promises" a short time after Nixon's return from Peking when he said, in response to news reporters' queries about the U.S.-ROC Defense Pact, that the "treaty will be kept." [4] Since that time, White House officials have reiterated numerous times that Taiwan would not be abandoned.

In short, there are contradictions and confusions in U.S. legal policy for which President Carter's recognition formula provides no answer. In fact Carter's acknowledgment that Taiwan is a part of China reverses the apparently evolving U.S. policy of recognizing two Chinas—if one is to take White House promises to Taiwan as meaningful in the context of detente with the PRC. It is also worth noting that before Carter's announcement we had an ambassador in Taipei and a "liaison officer" in Peking with ambassadorial status and rank.

If America's China policy is to be made understandable to Americans and fair to the people living on Taiwan, the legal setting and legal question needs clarification. At the very least, American decision-makers should try to discern Taiwan's true legal status.

The analysis that follows will examine Taiwan's legal status based upon three separate approaches: 1) the argument based on historical claims and treaties; 2) the definition of a nation-state in international law; and 3) the United Nations' definition of nation-state and specific evidence that might give support to or reject a bid by Taipei for self-determination.

Historical Claims

The earliest inhabitants of Taiwan were of Malay stock, not Chinese. Early Chinese historical records make reference to Taiwan as Liu Chiu (the same name now used for the Ryukyu Islands) and give no indication that Taiwan was part of China; rather, Taiwan was regarded as a tributary state in the same category with Thailand, Nepal, Burma, Vietnam, Laos and Korea. [5] The earliest Chinese immigration to Taiwan occurred more than a thousand years ago, though Chinese inhabited only coastal areas until the seventeenth century when the Ming Dynasty was overthrown and a remnant force fled to Taiwan with a number of followers. Until the eighteenth century, however, aborigines on the island probably still outnumbered Chinese. [6]

During the beginning of the colonial era, Taiwan came under foreign control and Peking made no protest. Also, until the mid-1600s, there were few contacts between Taiwan and China. When a Chinese government was established on Taiwan it was an exile government which never regained power in China; thus even after Chinese gained *de facto* rule over most of Taiwan, no contacts existed with China. Even after Peking conquered the remnants of the Ming loyalists that had fled to Taiwan, it did not establish effective political control there. Taiwan was regarded by China as a "land inhabited by barbarians," which to the Chinese—since China was a cultural concept and its borders were seen accordingly—made Taiwan an area not regarded as part of China. Furthermore, under Chinese law, since it was technically illegal to leave the country and those who did were denationalized, Chinese who fled to Taiwan were no longer considered Chinese.

During the seventeenth and eighteenth centuries, government in the Chinese-inhabited areas of Taiwan was under the control of local families. Most of the interior of the island was dominated by the aboriginal tribes, who negotiated various legal agreements including treaties with officials of European governments. [7] In the 1700s, foreign influence in Taiwan saw a marked upswing despite nominal ties with China, and in the 1800s, the United States government asked Peking if Taiwan was a part of China and received a negative reply. Cognizant of Taiwan's status, Commodore Perry recommended that the United States establish a protectorate status over Taiwan. The United States President decided against this—but for reasons that related to U.S. domestic politics. In 1874 an Okinawan ship ran aground on Taiwan and its crew was murdered by the aborigines. Japan protested this incident in Peking, but Peking disclaimed any responsibility on the grounds that the crime had not been committed "in its jurisdiction." [8]

In 1887 Taiwan was made a province of China, but this status lasted for only eight years—until the Sino-Japanese War when, by the Treaty of Shimonoseki, Peking ceded Taiwan to Japan "in perpetuity." At this time Taiwanese were given a two-year period during which they could opt for Chinese citizenship and return to China. Less than two-tenths of 1 per cent so chose. [9] Nor did the Taiwanese masses turn to China to try to keep Taiwan since, in the view of most Taiwanese, Taiwan was not part of China. As they saw it, Peking had had adequate time to make a move to incorporate Taiwan but did not. The Taiwanese blamed Peking for piracy and other problems in the

Taiwan area. Yet, the Taiwanese did not accept Japan's control either, and before Japan was able to set up jurisdiction over the island, the Taiwanese revolted and established the "Republic of Taiwan." Nevertheless, within months the Japanese pacified the island and for the next fifty years Taiwan was a Japanese colony. During this time Japanese was used in the education system, though Taiwanese customs and language were not extinguished. Weak ties with China were severed and immigration from China stopped. Taiwan experienced economic development under Japanese control that raised its standard of living well beyond that of China, while its economy became foreign-trade-oriented, attaining by 1938 nearly forty times the per capita trade volume of China. [10]

There is evidence that, during the period of Japanese control, many Taiwanese were pleased with the Japanese owing to the prosperity and social order they brought. Some parts of Taiwan remained outside Japanese control. These were not the Chinese-populated areas but, rather, mountainous areas inhabited by unfriendly aboriginal tribes. During World War II, U.S. military authorities drew up a plan to invade Taiwan but scrapped the plan when they realized that they could not count on local support against the Japanese. [11]

Also during World War II, China (both the Nationalists and the Communists) renounced the Treaty of Shimonoseki and other agreements with Japan. The legality of this move, however, is questionable as international law does not give the right of unilateral abrogation of a treaty with international status. In 1943, at Cairo, Roosevelt and Churchill promised President Chiang Kai-shek in a joint communique that all territory Japan had "stolen . . . such as . . . Taiwan . . . shall be restored to the Republic of China." This, however, only amounted to a declaration—with little status in international law. Moreover, it was in contradiction to provisions in the Atlantic Charter which declared that territorial changes not in accord with the freely expressed wishes of the people concerned are not valid. The Atlantic Charter both preceded and outranked the Cairo Declaration. It is also relevant that the Cairo "proclamations" on the United States' part did not have the support of Congress insofar as Roosevelt did not bring the matter before Congress. Nor did the United States ask for support on the provisions in the Cairo Declaration from its allies, many of whom were not concerned about the provisions and felt that the United States was unrealistic in trying to give China big power status. [12]

Nevertheless, at Potsdam, the provisions in the Cairo Declaration concerning Taiwan were repeated. No date was set for the transfer of Taiwan, nor was anything said in specific terms about the transfer. This was to await a formal peace treaty between Japan and the Allies. It should also be noted that although the number of participants at Potsdam was more than at Cairo, and although the significance of this conference was greater than that of the Cairo meeting in view of the impending Japanese collapse and the fact that a surrender agreement and a peace treaty were to be signed soon, the product of the Potsdam Conference was still only a declaration.

Before a peace treaty was signed, however, Nationalist Chinese authorities assumed jurisdiction over Taiwan, authorized to do so by General MacArthur as Supreme Commander of Allied Forces in the Pacific and as a trustee on behalf of the Allied powers. Upon the arrival of the Nationalist Chinese Army, the Japanese colonial government left and returned to Japan. Four years later, in 1949, the Nationalist Chinese were defeated on the mainland by Communist military forces. Remnants of the Nationalist Army plus a large number of government officials fled to Taiwan where they set up a government-in-exile. In 1951, the Allies—with the exception of the Communist countries, which objected to Washington's unilateral management of the occupation of Japan and the presence of U.S. forces there—signed a peace treaty with Japan. In this treaty, Japan formally renounced any claim to Taiwan and the Pescadores—though the treaty did not say to whom the transfer of territory was made, and, in fact, left the issue of ownership ambiguous. Some articles of the treaty refer to the Republic of China and do not suggest territorial limits; other articles speak of the Republic of China as limited to Taiwan and the Pescadores. Still other portions of the treaty use the term China without reference to which China. [13]

Neither Peking nor Taipei were signatories of the treaty, though Japan the next year signed a bilateral treaty with the ROC ending the state of war. Article II of this treaty reiterated Japan's renouncement of all right, title and claim to Taiwan and the Penghu (Pescadores) Islands, hinting that Tokyo was giving territorial claim to Taiwan and the Pescadores to the ROC. This view can be strengthened by adding to it the argument that, inasmuch as Japan had abandoned or had given up sovereignty over Taiwan, then legal claim to the territory could be made on the basis of occupation and control. In 1954 the United States signed a treaty of defense with the Republic of China, citing Taiwan and the Pescadores, but again no mention was made of the legal status of this territory.

Meanwhile Peking laid legal claim to Taiwan on the basis of Taiwan being historically part of China. As we have already seen, however, the argument that Taiwan is historically part of China is dubious. The PRC's historical claim, moreover, was further weakened by a statement Mao made in 1936 which indicated that he did not regard Taiwan as part of China, and similar statements made thereafter by other top Chinese Communist leaders. [14] In any event, a historical claim usually gives way to other legal arguments or to occupation. This clearly seemed the case here.

Peking also claimed Taiwan as its territory on the basis of it being the legal successor government to the ROC. There are similarly serious legal difficulties with this argument. First of all, the ROC still exists; therefore, the PRC cannot be said to be its successor particularly where Taiwan is concerned. Furthermore, inasmuch as the PRC has declared the San Francisco Treaty "illegal," it cannot claim Taiwan on the basis of the transfer of Taiwan made by Japan to the ROC, or to themselves assuming that they should have been the party to receive Taiwan. A similar problem exists in attempting to make a claim based on the Cairo or Potsdam declarations since both specified that Taiwan would be returned to the ROC—signifying a specific regime. Likewise the argument used by the PRC that World War II automatically voided the Treaty of Shimonoseki and that Taiwan became a part of China in 1941 is not legally sound as the precedent of the transfer of Alsace and Lorraine after World War I indicates. Finally, the argument of successorship is further weakened by the fact that the ROC has entered into a number of agreements that would be found binding by any international legal authority, and which specify Taiwan and the Pescadores as their realm of jurisdiction—thus making it possible to view the ROC not as a replaced regime, but rather one that moved from China to Taiwan and is now the legal government of the latter only.

Until the Shanghai Communique the United States appeared to espouse the position that Taiwan was not a part of China, at least in the sense that its legal status had not been determined. In 1950, President Truman made reference to Taiwan by stating that for the past four years the United States and the other allied powers have "accepted the exercise of Chinese authority over the island." [15] Had he assumed that Taiwan was a part of China he would have used different terms. In 1954 the United States signed a mutual defense treaty with the ROC, but put this provision in the treaty: "nothing in the present treaty shall be construed as affecting or modifying the legal status or the sovereignty of Formosa and the Pescadores." Subsequently, Secretary of State John Foster Dulles declared that "sovereignty over Formosa and the Pescadores has never been settled." He noted that both the Japanese peace treaty signed with the allies and the separate agreement signed with the ROC did not specify Taiwan's legal status. He went on to state that the status of Taiwan and the Pescadores is different than the offshore islands, which he said "have always been Chinese territory." [16] This could be construed to mean that Taiwan was not part of China. Later, during the Eisenhower Administration and also when Presidents Kennedy and Johnson were in office, U.S. policy seemed to be evolving toward a "two Chinas policy" or more precisely a "one China and one Taiwan policy." This was also true in the Nixon Administration, seen in statements by Secretary of State Rogers before Nixon went to China.

The Shanghai Communique must therefore be seen as a sincere attempt to further detente with Peking without appreciably changing Washington's stance on Taiwan's legal status—which, of course, was difficult because Peking had already made it clear that the Taiwan issue was the major obstacle to improving relations and had said that it would not deal with the United States "until Taiwan had been restored." The wording, as already noted, certainly affords ambiguity, presumably the only avenue open to the negotiators. One would hardly conclude that "does not challenge" indicates that the United States agreed that Taiwan belongs to the PRC. Peking may wish to take this view, and, as has already been pointed out, the Chinese translation makes such an interpretation easier. It is also noteworthy that at the time the Shanghai Communique was signed it was reported that Henry Kissinger wanted to use the words "accept" rather than "does not challenge," and "all Chinese" for "Chinese on either side of the Taiwan Strait." [17] Thus it appears that President Nixon or other members of the delegation, or both, opposed making a statement that supported Peking's claim to ownership of Taiwan, and they won out in terms of the final wording of the agreement. This is confirmed by Assistant Secretary of State Marshall Green's statement a month later that the status of Taiwan is "undetermined." [18]

Taiwan as a Nation-State

A majority of scholars of international law agree that the definition of nation-state includes the following: 1) a defined territory; 2) a permanent population; 3) a government; 4) the capacity to enter into relations with other states. These provisions, which were accepted by most legal scholars in the last century were formalized in the Montevideo Convention in 1933, to which the United States was a signatory. If any trend is discernible since 1933 in international law or in U.S. practice, it is to regard these criteria with greater flexibility than originally intended and to give them a broader interpretation.

The Republic of China's physical size amounts to nearly 14,000 square miles, which includes Taiwan and some small islands around Taiwan. Although the ROC makes claim to all of China—plus outer Mongolia, territory in the Soviet Union, Japan and a number of Southeast Asian countries—the territory under its control has remained almost unchanged since 1949. The ROC also claims jurisdiction in the Taiwan Strait based upon its claim to the mainland, but, Taipei has not gone beyond what international law would define as its rights as a separate nation-state in setting guidelines for passage of ships or in granting drilling rights for oil and natural gas in the area. Furthermore, the ROC has entered into a number of treaties which specify that its territory is limited to the area under its control—not including China—and thus seems to have allowed for at least a temporary separation between Taiwan and China.

The United States has entered into agreements with the ROC which also specify that its territory is limited to Taiwan and the Pescadores, or "territory under its control." This includes the U.S.-ROC Mutual Defense Treaty of 1954, which defined in Article VI the territory of the ROC to mean Taiwan and the Pescadores. The United States Congress subsequently passed the Formosa Resolution which gave the President the authority to use military force to defend the offshore islands, but this has since been rescinded. In any case, neither in making this pledge, nor in nullifying it, was the U.S. position on the ROC's territorial status altered. Other agreements that the United States entered into with the ROC generally include the definition of ROC territory to include only Taiwan and the Pescadores—the same territory which according to historical and treaty arguments seems not to be a part of China.

Inasmuch as the ROC's physical size makes it larger than a majority of the legally recognized nation-states in the world and that the territory under its control has not changed in any important way in the past nearly thirty years, it would pass the territorial test of nation-state status easily. On the other hand, this must be seen in the context of the PRC's claim to ROC territory and the fact that the ROC's legitimacy is strong or weak in some part based on the PRC's claim. The fact that the offshore islands have been bombarded regularly since 1958 by PRC forces, together with the fact that the ROC has abandoned some of them, would appear to put them in a different category than Taiwan and the Pescadores, or in the status of contested or disputed territory. [19] The legal argument called "international prescription," that a state of things which has existed for a long time should be changed as little as possible, would seem to substantiate the claim that the ROC should remain in control of Taiwan and the Pescadores, though this would probably not be true of the offshore islands. Peking has also made claim from the point of view of prescription but this is based on the historical argument which, as we have already seen in the discussion concerning historical claims, has little strength.

The PRC has also made a claim based on occupative title and contiguous title. The former argument goes as follows. During the period of colonization, European powers acquired territory by gaining sovereignty through force and by maintaining effective control. Inasmuch as Peking, during the colonial period, repudiated jurisdiction over Taiwan and held real control over it for such a brief time this argument is hardly convincing. Furthermore, Peking has contradicted its own argument by saying that the reason Taiwan is not under its control is "American imperialism." Thus, using the notion of occupative title, an argument might also be made that Taiwan belongs to the United States—at least following Peking's line of argument.

Another argument, called contiguous title, is based on the proximity of Taiwan to China and was given some support in 1958 by extending the area of legitimate claim to the continental shelf. The problem with this argument is that Taiwan is too far away from China to make a strong claim—ninety miles at the closest point. Moreover, using this argument, part of Japan, all of the Ryukyu Islands, and part or all of the Philippines could belong to China. Alternatively, since there is a closer geographical relationship between Taiwan and Japan (assuming Japan is not part of the mainland), Taiwan could be viewed as a part of Japan.

In the context of discussing U.S. China policy, it is particularly important to note that the U.S. interpretation of international law clearly seems to favor the ROC's legal jurisdiction over Taiwan or an undetermined status, rather than any of the PRC's arguments. Furthermore, it can be added that Washington's actions relative to American companies exploring for oil offshore around Taiwan and its assumptions about the Taiwan Strait being an international waterway, both of which have current application, seem to favor a Taiwan detached from China.

The ROC has a population of 17 million, nearly all of which resides on the island of Taiwan and which, since 1949, has been stable in terms of emigration and immigration. The size of the ROC's population would clearly give it nation-state status inasmuch as three-fourths of the members of the United Nations are smaller.

Since one of the central arguments used by the PRC for claiming Taiwan is based on the fact that its residents are Chinese, the so-called racial suzerainty argument must be given closer scrutiny. PRC spokesmen have noted, for example, that the majority of the population of Taiwan migrated from China and that they still speak Chinese languages, primarily the dialect spoken around Amoy (Fukien province) and Mandarin, which is the official language in both the PRC and the ROC. This kind of claim has had no acceptance in international legal circles for some time and is generally regarded as an antiquated facet of international law that was supplanted by more democratic and humane interpretations in the mid-nineteenth century. The democratic trend in international law makes such a claim in modern times even weaker.

The requirement of a government for nation-state status generally refers to political stability and effective rule. Based on the criterion of stability, the ROC would clearly qualify for nation-state status. It is one of the most stable polities among developing countries. The ROC has experienced no irregular transfers of executive authority since it was established on Taiwan and would rank very low in terms of threats against the government, riots, and crime. The ROC government also maintains a large military organization that provides adequate security over the area that it governs. There have been no serious internal challenges to the government in almost thirty years.

In recent years the legal definition of stable government has more and more related to mass support for the nation's leadership. It is uncertain how much mass support the ROC regime has, and one can assume that there are many Taiwanese who would like either to overthrow the government or have Taiwanese represented in the government more than they are now. On the other hand, the Nationalist Party, which in the past had few Taiwanese members, is now 60 to 80 per cent Taiwanese. [20] And though they are not yet very well represented at the top, there has been a marked improvement since 1972 when Chiang Ching-kuo became Premier. The position of Vice-President, about a third of the Cabinet, and most Provincial Assembly seats are now held by Taiwanese. It is also important to note that as the threat of incorporation by the PRC became more imminent, after Taiwan lost membership in the United Nations and President Nixon went to China and signed the Shanghai Communique, Peking made both propositions and threats toward the ROC and there was less opposition to the government by Taiwanese and more unity among the two major "ethnic" groups in Taiwan. For a while, Peking made a special appeal to the Taiwanese to withhold support from the ROC government, but there was little response and this tactic was abandoned. [21]

A democratic system of government or democratic practices are also criteria used to measure the amount of mass support for the government. Although the ROC government is based on a one-party system, the Nationalist Party, or Kuomintang (KMT), is a mass party and has a larger membership per capita than most parties, including the Communist Party in the PRC.

[22] And while elections have not been contested seriously by other parties (there are two small opposition parties), the number of independent candidates has increased in recent years. In the 1977 election, independent candidates won 15 per cent of the seats in the Provincial Assembly. This has led some to describe the system as "one party plus independents." The registration of voters and voter turnout also suggest that democracy has evolved in the ROC. In the 1977 election, 80 per cent of the qualified voters cast ballots. [23]

Regarding the need for external or diplomatic relations to qualify for nation-state status, several important trends need to be assessed. Clearly the ROC has lost diplomatic status in recent years, in terms of official diplomatic relations or embassies in Taipei. It is no longer a member of the United Nations nor of most UN affiliate organizations. On the other hand, the ROC's past record and its ability to compensate for recent diplomatic setbacks may give it sufficient ties to qualify for nation-state status. From 1949 to 1965, the ROC had more support for representing China in the United Nations than the PRC. On the other hand, the trend favored the PRC—up to 1965. After 1965, the trend reversed itself temporarily, though by 1970 the PRC finally had more votes in the United Nations than the ROC. Then, in 1971, the two-thirds vote requirement was voted down by a four-vote margin and Peking was admitted. At that time, 35 nations voted for the ROC's right to hold the China seat and 17 abstained.

The same situation applies to diplomatic recognition. The ROC prevailed through the 1950s and early 1960s. In 1966, the ROC still had 60 embassies abroad as opposed to Peking's 50, with 21 nations recognizing neither. And the ROC maintained its lead up to 1971. In 1977, the ROC had recognition from only 23 nations, but it had won recognition from some newly independent nations—Tonga and Western Samoa.

The ROC, then, may still qualify as a nation-state because of its remaining official diplomatic ties with some 23 nations at the ambassadorial level. Nor can membership in the

United Nations be used as a requirement for nation-state status as no one has questioned the legitimacy of Switzerland, a non-member. Finally, the loss of recognition and a seat in the United Nations has not affected the ROC's treaty status very much; Taipei still has thousands of treaties with other nations in force.

And although the ROC was expelled from the United Nations and a number of its affiliate organizations, Taipei is still represented in the International Monetary Fund, the World Bank and the Asian Development Bank. The PRC has demanded ROC expulsion from these organizations, but due to the weighted voting in the IMF and the World Bank according to contributions, the PRC may not be able to get the votes required to oust the ROC. In addition, the ROC owes $310 million to the World Bank, which is hesitant to admit the PRC unless it is willing to take over this debt. Other organizations such as global scientific organizations, the International Red Cross and the International Olympic Committee (IOC) claim to be non-political and thus their membership is open to citizens rather than governments. These organizations have also refused to expel ROC representatives. The IOC and Canada became embroiled in a controversy at the Olympic games in 1976, which resulted in neither China participating. In addition, some of the "political" international organizations, affiliated with the United Nations through UNESCO, have not as yet expelled Taipei and some have resisted. In some others the ROC participates despite its lack of membership. For example, the ROC was expelled from the International Telecommunications Satellite Organization, but is still allowed to use their facilities. Taipei also lost membership in the International Atomic Energy Agency, though its representatives still inspect Taiwan's nuclear power sites. [24]

And while the ROC lost official diplomatic relations during the period 1971-1976, it has been able to compensate for this to a great extent with other forms of contacts, often by cleverly conceived methods which work almost the same as diplomatic ties. Furthermore, during the period when Taipei suffered its most serious diplomatic losses, with embassies leaving

Taipei almost monthly, its trade with all of the nations that left increased, in many cases by considerable margins. In fact, Taiwan's overall trade increased nearly fourfold during this so-called "bleak" period. Similarly the number of foreigners visiting Taiwan increased by 50 per cent each year during this period. [25] This was in large part the product of the ROC's special efforts to maintain foreign contacts, but it also represents the willingness of nations to deal with Taiwan in spite of their new ties with the PRC, and perhaps, in the case of many, an effort to help Taipei maintain its independence by increasing trade and other contacts.

The ROC has also set up a number of informal organizations to manage its external affairs in the absence of diplomatic ties. In 1970 it created the China External Trade Development Council (CETDC), which supplanted the commercial attaches and official trade missions lost with official diplomatic ties. This organization has a variety of names overseas, ranging from the Oficina Comercial de Taiwan, in Buenos Aires, to the CETDC Correspondent in Australia, to the Far East Trading Company in Canada. Where the term "China" presents any problem, the title Far East Trade Service, Inc. has been used. Trade and other economic contacts have thus been maintained and increased, and to date Taiwanese businessmen have had little trouble traveling, attending meetings abroad, etc. [26] In some cases visas have to be obtained in third countries, but this can often be done by mail and simply requires an extra two or three days lead time. In many other places airline representatives give visas. Many formerly official transactions are thus fulfilled on an unofficial basis.

All of this, however, had been made easier by the presence of the United States in Taipei and the ROC's official presence in the United States, both of which reflected U.S. support for Taipei. Now that the United States has recognized the PRC, the mode by which this will be done involves additional legal problems which will no doubt affect the ROC's external ties, both formal and informal.

It should also be noted that the ROC's news representatives have generally maintained their presence abroad, in spite of

Peking's efforts to have them expelled wherever Peking has a presence. It is also worthwhile noting that the official Soviet news agency TASS on one occasion since 1971 referred to Taiwan as a "nation" and that the ROC's trade and other unofficial contacts with most of the East European countries have increased.

United Nations Practice on Taiwan

United Nations practice, as it relates to legal title to territory, generally takes the historical argument to be a weak one. [27] Likewise, wartime declarations—and the Cairo and Potsdam proclamations are no exception—are generally seen as propaganda statements and are thus not regarded as binding. It should also be noted in this connection that the United Nations Charter (Article CIII) states that "in the event of a conflict between . . . the present Charter and their obligations under any other international agreement . . . obligations under . . . the Charter shall prevail." Thus according to UN usage, the arguments concerning Taiwan's legal status must be presented in terms of currently relevant arguments without giving much weight to the historical claims or the wartime agreements and proclamations; i.e., the present situation prevails.

In terms of defining nationhood or nation-state status, United Nations practice is very liberal and the ROC would no doubt qualify easily, although this point needs to be argued. Nation-state status is generally conferred by membership in the United Nations or other international organizations. Inasmuch as the ROC was a member of the United Nations up to 1971, it clearly had nation-state status at that time. It could not, however, be argued, that the ROC lost its nation-state status because it lost United Nations membership in 1971, as the case of Indonesia, which left the United Nations in 1965 and later rejoined, suggests. In fact, the United Nations seemed to hold Indonesia's membership in abeyance, since Djarkata did not have to go through the same procedures as new members when it rejoined. The fact that the ROC's debt to the United Nations was not taken over by the PRC and has not been cancelled suggests that the ROC may hold residual United Nations membership or may be able to rejoin under different procedures than new nations— even though in practical terms this is impossible because the PRC would veto the membership application. Furthermore, the United Nations regards Switzerland and other nations that do not hold United Nations membership as fully legal nation-states.

UN practice also suggests that nation-state status is attained by taking membership in other international organizations inasmuch as the United Nations has listed participants in other world organizations along with United Nations members in most United Nations publications and documents. Since the ROC still belongs to a number of world organizations it might be concluded that it has some, if not considerable, legal status accrued in this way.

United Nations qualifications for nationhood are intentionally minimal, so as to make the world body truly universal. This even applies to pseudo-nations such as the Ukraine SSR and Byelorussia SSR—obviously nonautonomous provinces of the USSR. One might conclude, then, that since the only major states not members are the two Koreas and Taiwan (in addition to Switzerland which has rejected membership), they should be persuaded into applying for membership in the future and that the present United Nations membership should grant them participation. Only in this way will the nation-state system become universal—which clearly seems to be the United Nations' intent.

By analyzing United Nations practice with reference to the ROC's legal status and the future of its territory and population, it becomes clear that the status of both are undetermined. Resolution 2758, by which the PRC was admitted to the United Nations, simply "restored the rights" of the PRC. The resolution, and likewise discussions held at the time, did not say that Taiwan is a part of China nor that the PRC has any legal claim to territory under the present jurisdiction of the ROC. And nothing was said about the ROC's legal status when it departed from the United Nations. Rather, the United Nations was silent in these matters and what happened was simply the replacement of one regime by another. One might conclude from this that the United Nations was unable to admit both Chinas, and therefore chose one; and since it did not say anything about the future status of the ROC or the territory or population under its jurisdiction, the hope or expectation may have been that the ROC should re-apply for membership or the people and the territory it controls should apply under another title.

It is noteworthy that the United States took the position at the time that the ROC should retain membership, but lost on this issue. Nonetheless, the nations that voted against the U.S. position and for the admission of Peking did not go further and declare the ROC's territory as belonging to the PRC.

Finally, delineating the statements made by members of the United Nations in UN sessions where the issue of Taiwan was discussed also gives evidence that the United Nations' view is that Taiwan's status is yet to be determined, and that Peking does not have legal claim. For example, even though the UK voted for seating Peking in the United Nations, its delegates have consistently stated that sovereignty over the island is undetermined. The position taken by most other European countries is similar or identical with the British position, though this was not usually cited at the time of voting. In many cases this can be assumed, however, because the United Nations vote came at the time that a number of member nations granted diplomatic recognition to the PRC. Most governments, following the examples of Canada and Italy, simply "took note" of Peking's claim.

The position that the ROC is an illegitimate government and that its territory is purely a matter of domestic jurisdiction for the PRC is strengthened by President Carter's decision to recognize Peking. But this position, however, is definitely not in accord with United Nations practice. In the United Nations the legitimacy of a government is not subject to another regime's influence, but is to be decided by the right of self-determination. The argument that the issue is a domestic one would be further rejected by international lawyers, particularly those working with the United Nations, who note that in almost all contests over territory, one party tries to make its claim a domestic issue and that this approach should as a matter of course be rejected.

The principle of nonacquisition of territory by force is also maintained by the United Nations. Thus, when Peking states that it will "liberate Taiwan by military force if necessary," as it has said several times, it is clearly in opposition to a basic United Nations principle. This principle may be one of the most potent ideals of the United Nations. It should also be noted that the United Nations has employed force to uphold this position and that the United States supports the United Nations' interpretation.

In the event that in any "dangerous" situation, whether involving a territorial claim or the legitimacy of a regime or not, if there is a threat to peace the United Nations can claim jurisdiction. Therefore, the PRC would be in violation of the Charter if it takes military action against the ROC, inasmuch as it has agreed to settle disputes by peaceful means and refrain in international relations from the use of force (Article II). And the Charter specifically states that this applies to nonmembers, whether they are committing aggressions or are the threatened parties. Even though Peking argues that this is a domestic matter and thus is not within United Nations jurisdiction, this could hardly be taken seriously; an effort to use force against Taiwan (if the ROC resisted) would create an incident with international ramifications. The military capabilities of the ROC underscore the point.

Probably the strongest United Nations position on the legal definition of the nation-state, and the one most applicable to the Taiwan issue, is its emphasis on the requirement of self-determination to ascertain nation-state status. The principle of self-determination is stated in Article I of the United Nations Charter and its importance in United Nations legal philosophy can be demonstrated in a variety of other ways. The International Covenant on Economic, Social and Cultural Rights and the International Covenant on Civil and Political Rights, both adopted by the General Assembly in 1966, reiterate the principle of self-determination and give this right to "all people." Although the strength of this concept stems from the anticolonial movement, it seems to have clear application in the case of Taiwan. Until 1945 Taiwan was a colonial territory, at which time the ROC became the "caretaker authority." Its status was left unresolved even after Japan signed a peace treaty with the Allies. Thus Taiwan could be placed in the same category as other territories that Japan relinquished—which were placed under United Nations jurisdiction as non-self-governing territories. Hence it would appear that the right of self-determination applies.

Self-determination is also a popular goal of the world body. And the United States has supported this concept enthusiastically, as reflected in its efforts to speed up the decolonization movement and to grant all territories their independence, including those under United Nations trusteeship and even those under U.S. jurisdiction. The rule of consistency as well as justice would thus give the people of Taiwan, should the ROC choose to exercise this option, the right of self-determination with both UN and U.S. support. In this context it is important to point out that both the United Nations and the Carter Administration's human rights campaign underscore this right. Hence the legal bearing of the right to self-determination has become stronger in the last few years and should have an even greater impact on the resolution of the Taiwan question than it would otherwise.

A final tenet of UN thinking on the legal requirements of nation-state status is the concept of democracy or mass support: the right of plebiscite. It is plain from United Nations practice that the preferred nation-state is not only one that grants its citizens human rights, but also one that gives them a voice in government. Hence, the best way of deciding the fate of populated territories where its legal status is in question is to use the plebiscite. Article LXXVI (b) of the United Nations Charter relates directly to the question of determining the fate of trust territories and appears applicable. It has application to Taiwan whether or not it is seen as a trust territory. For example, the United Nations sent representatives to assess the wishes of the people in Malaysia in 1963 and Bahrain in 1970. In addition, the United Nations supervised elections in the Cook Islands in 1965 and in Equatorial Guinea in 1968. It gave its support to a French-sponsored plebiscite in Algeria in 1962 and conducted one itself in West Irian.

Again, United States policy on this facet of United Nations practice has been one of full support. In all of the cases mentioned above Washington gave its enthusiastic approval. Moreover, the United States has employed the plebiscite itself in deciding the fate of territory under its jurisdiction. In 1972 the United States returned Okinawa and the rest of the Ryukyu Islands to Japan based on a plebiscite. In 1977 it used a plebiscite to decide the future of some of the Pacific islands and promised that future changes in status there would be handled the same way.

Conclusions

From the above discussion it is clear that the PRC does not have a strong case for claiming any territory under the ROC's jurisdiction, except for the offshore islands. None of the arguments mentioned—historical and treaty claims, the traditional definition of the nation-state, or United Nations usage—renders the verdict that the dispute is a domestic one. Rather, it confirms that the ROC is an independent, sovereign nation-state. Furthermore, as United Nations practice becomes more widespread and accepted as a foundation for legal practice, the historical and treaty arguments will weaken still further, and the present situation and wishes of the residents of Taiwan should become more crucial deciding factors.

It is clear that until December 15, 1978 the United States had never given any indication (with the exception of the ambiguously worded Shanghai Communique) that Taiwan is the territory of the PRC, or for that matter that it is part of China. President Carter, however, recognized "the government of the People's Republic" as the "sole legal government of China." He also acknowledged that Taiwan is a part of China. This was an anomaly. Previously the United States has provided enthusiastic backing for both the traditional views and UN practice on the status of territorial claims and on the methods to resolve territorial disputes. The United States has also supported plebiscites to resolve jurisdictional problems and has stood for self-determination. Washington's pressure on the ROC to adopt democratic institutions and enlist mass support for policy decisions, including recent proddings by the Carter Administration for Taipei to hold freer elections, suggests that the United States expected free choice to play a role in the fate of Taiwan.

If a plebiscite is offered, it is easy to guess how the residents of the Republic of China will choose. The alternatives to independence are 1) becoming a part of China, 2) United Nations jurisdiction, or 3) ties with the United States, the Soviet Union or Japan. Although the majority of the people living on Taiwan would no doubt prefer a truly independent state (a Republic of Taiwan), there is at present no popular organized opposition to the ROC government. Furthermore, Taiwanese are rapidly winning proportional representation, making independence mean independence both for Taiwanese and Mainlanders and an ultimate assimilation of the latter by the former. Finally, the crucial issue for both Taiwanese and Mainland Chinese residing on Taiwan is Peking's claim to Taiwan and its threats to "liberate" Taiwan. Only a few radical Taiwanese put the conflict between themselves and the Mainlanders in a higher priority than maintaining Taiwan's freedom and autonomy.

The United States, in an effort to seek better relations with Peking in the context of growing PRC-Soviet hostilities, said in the Shanghai Communique that it "does not challenge" the view that there is only one China. This is very different from President Carter's December 1978 acknowledgment that Taiwan is a part of China. This hasty decision to concede to Peking's territorial claims to Taiwan will contribute to undermining the legal structure of world politics and United Nations practice unless reversed in coming years.

Chapter Four
HUMAN RIGHTS: "THE SOUL OF AMERICAN FOREIGN POLICY"

In his December 15 announcement of the recognition President Carter had stated only days before that the issue of of the People's Republic of China, President Carter stated that normalization would not jeopardize the well-being of the people of Taiwan. "They face a peaceful and prosperous future," he said. [1] However, Carter did not mention personal freedoms nor the impact of his action on human rights in either Taiwan or the PRC. This omission seemed unusual in view of the fact that human rights is the "soul of American foreign policy." Moreover, an effort to promote the cause of human rights has been flaunted as a main principle of the Carter Administration's foreign policy since he took office, and the President has asserted on numerous occasions that his foreign policy differs from those of previous Presidents in this way.

Apparently the issue of human rights had almost no role in formulating a new China policy. Following President Carter's recognition statement, Patricia M. Derian, Assistant Secretary of State for Human Rights and Humanitarian Affairs, revealed that before normalization was achieved, the issue of human rights had only been "discussed" with the PRC. [2] Though we do not know how significant this discussion was, one can easily infer the role of human rights in our new China policy by taking note of the statement made by Teng Hsiao-ping, China's Deputy Prime Minister, before his visit to this country that "it is wrong to make human rights a subject for discussion with the United States." [3]

In fact, President Carter justified his recognition of the PRC in terms bereft of morality by saying that "we are recognizing simple reality." However, it should be noted that having made human rights an issue in our relations with many countries, especially the Soviet Union, the obvious lack of consideration for human rights in our relations with the PRC would make many believe that the U.S. human rights campaign is selective in scope. The different treatment of Moscow and Peking on the human rights issue suggests a U.S. "tilt" toward the PRC, an impression the U.S. wants to avoid.

The foreign policy of the United States has long been influenced by a deep philosophical commitment to human rights and concern for human rights is not new with the Carter Administration. It is expressed in the first ten amendments of the Constitution and in the principles of human freedom and self-determination as reflected by America's central role in writing the UN Charter and Universal Declaration of Human Rights. American foreign-policymakers have also long assumed that a legitimate government must be founded upon the consent of the governed, and that basic human freedoms must be a paramount goal of all national leaders. It is assumed that universally accepted standards of human rights can offer relief to a world locked in conflict. Thus, what we do or fail to do with respect to human rights will have much influence on the degree of freedom enjoyed in tomorrow's world.

Human rights constitute a list of desirable domestic political arrangements which maximize the personal freedom of individual human beings, but the human rights vocabulary, and hence measurement, is marked by ambiguity. When asked how American standards can be applied to countries that have a different concept of human rights, Assistant Secretary Derian replied by saying that "the Universal Declaration of Human Rights—recognized by the U.N. General Assembly—is well known to people, and they subscribe to it. There are certain universally accepted human rights that are recognized throughout the world." [4]

The Universal Declaration of Human Rights and its two related Covenants are widely accepted yardsticks which enumerate the rights every human being should enjoy as criteria with which to assess the status of human rights on both sides of the

Taiwan Strait. After all, the Declaration should be "a common standard of achievement for all peoples of all nations" as Carter pointed out in his 1978 speech observing the 30th anniversary of the Declaration. Furthermore, the PRC, now one of the permanent members in the Security Council of the UN, and the ROC, a founding member of the UN, are both endorsers of the Declaration. The various freedoms and rights enumerated in those documents come under the following categories:

(1) Equality before the law.

(2) Due process of law, which includes the rights of not being held in slavery or subjected to torture or cruel punishment and the right to a fair trial by an independent tribunal.

(3) Freedom of movement and residence within each state and freedom to emigrate.

(4) Freedom of religion.

(5) Freedom of peaceful assembly and association.

(6) Freedom of thought, belief, speech and expression; i.e., to seek, receive and impart information and ideas.

(7) Right to an adequate standard of living, privacy, education, employment, social welfare and security, to take part in cultural life, etc.

(8) Right of self-determination.

Within this framework let us now review the human rights situation in the PRC and the ROC. The right of self-determination was discussed separately due to the special relevance of this important right to the future of Taiwan.

Human Rights in the PRC

The PRC is ruled by the Chinese Communist Party, which is the supreme authority in China. Its rule is called the "dictatorship of the proletariat" and is based on the tenets of Marxism-Leninism and Mao Tse-tung thought. Three decades after the 1949 revolution, systemic and "legal" discrimination against "class enemies" (i.e., landlords) is still carried on. In fact, deprivation of political rights of the "class enemies" has its basis in the Constitution. [5] According to Mao's own estimate, approximately 5 per cent of the Chinese population are defined as "class enemies." [6] This implies that the political rights of 50 million people are abused just because they used to be the landlords or rich peasants, or simply because their parents were. These people are systematically deprived of the right to higher education, certain categories of jobs and the right to live in specific cities and areas of China.

There are no legal remedies to redress the adverse consequences of those of bad "class background" because the "due process of law" does not exist in the PRC. As one Chinese newspaper recently admitted, the legal system is in disorder. In an article by the Law School of the Academy of Social Sciences, it is argued that due to the lack of a criminal code and the incompleteness of legal process, there are no concrete legal bases to define crimes and no specific criteria to punish criminals; the difference between the "guilty" and "not guilty" is sometimes blurred and frequently the innocent are punished and the guilty not brought to justice. The article points out that there are many administrative as well as judicial organs that "capriciously" put people under arrest. Further, the arrested may be tortured or detained for a long period without any investigation, prosecution or trial. Additionally, according to the article, the rights of the defendant to defend and appeal are disallowed by some judicial organs. [7]

Such a "verdict" of the PRC's legal system can be confirmed by reports made by Amnesty International, a private organization that won the Nobel Peace Prize in 1977 for its campaigns on behalf of political prisoners around the world. Citing case histories of prisoners in China, Amnesty International [8] was "particularly concerned" about the following:

(1) Laws so loosely worded that "large scale imprisonment on political grounds has been permitted, that certain people are deprived of their political and civil rights on the basis of their 'class origin.'"

(2) Arrests on political grounds carried out during mass mobilization campaigns—thus broadening the range of political offenses defining new types of offenders according to the political necessities.

(3) The detention of political offenders for long periods before a trial and no formal guarantee of the right to defense. Detention is often used to compel offenders to write confessions before they are brought to trial. Trials are usually held either in secret or in mass public forums where no defense is possible.

(4) Punishment of political offenders without a judicial investigation. Such offenders are not brought before a court of justice but are assigned, as convicted prisoners are, to compulsory labor under special control.

(5) Conditions of detention facilities in violation of Chinese law for the maintenance of prisons and retention of some political prisoners against their will to work in penal establishments after their prison terms.[9]

A study done by Freedom House in 1978, found that in the PRC "all court cases are explicitly decided in political terms (there is no legal code); decisions are often capricious." It is also reported that there may be millions of political prisoners in China, including those in labor camps. [10]

According to one estimate, from 1949 to 1971, the direct cost in human lives in China has come to the staggering figure of between 30 million and 50 million which includes: political purges (1949-1958), 15-30 million; the "Great Leap Forward" movement and "People's Commune" program, 1-2 million; fighting minority nationalities (Tibetans included), .5-1 million; the Cultural Revolution and its aftermath, .25-.5 million; and deaths resulting from forced labor camps and frontier exploration, 15-25 million. [11] Though presumably a large proportion of these people were not directly executed by the PRC, the policies made or condoned by Peking are responsible for the loss of these lives.

For most of the people living under Peking's rule, freedom to travel abroad is unthinkable. The PRC even limits the freedom of travel of its people within its borders. The food ration system facilitates control of domestic travel. Since only those permitted to travel can exchange their local coupons for national food coupons, long-distance internal travel is nearly impossible for those who do not have approval.

Moreover, the *hsia-fang* policy of forcibly sending youth down to the countryside since 1968 has deprived more than 16 million people of the freedom to choose their place of residence. And this is not simply an occasional policy implemented in an emergency situation. It is a policy that has been practiced in China since the 1950s and is still used. Freedom of movement and residence are rights that are violated in a variety of other ways. For example, cadres in charge of discipline use mandatory transfers, especially those that separate husbands and wives or children, as a means of keeping discipline as well as a means of birth control. Those who are less politically aware are transferred for similar reasons. Because ration cards are not nationally standard, travel is in another way controlled. The same goes for the limited issuance of travel documents and permission from cadres before citizens can move or travel.

Freedom of religion is most precarious under the rule of the Chinese Communists. In the 1950s, religious persecution forced thousands of foreign missionaries to leave China. During the Cultural Revolution temples, churches, and mosques were destroyed or changed into factories and meeting halls. Religious artifacts and books were also destroyed. Since the downfall of the "Gang of Four," some religious activities have been permitted so as to improve China's human rights image but religious freedom applies only to foreigners.

In the PRC most assemblies and associations are State-Party-directed, and true freedom of assembly and association does not exist. Though spontaneous mass assemblies seem to be tolerated today, as being shown by the wall posters campaign in Peking recently, the Tien An Men demonstration of April 5, 1976 is a contradictory case in point. At Tien An Men a mass rally gathering to pay respects to the late Chou En-lai was violently broken up. Three thousand were arrested on the spot, more than one hundred killed, and more than forty thousand arrested and subjected to inhumane treatment. [12]

There has been periodic persecution of intellectuals and discrimination applied against applicants into institutions of higher learning and employment in education at all levels. After the Hundred Flowers Campaign in the mid-1950s, intellectuals were forced to criticize the government and the Party. They charged the Chinese Communist Party with arrogance, class consciousness and arbitrariness. In retaliation the Party cut funds for higher education and research and punished many scientists. This was repeated during the Great Proletarian Cultural Revolution (1965-1969) when anyone possessing higher education was suspect and condemned. In one year (1967), 3,000 members of the prestigious Academy of Science were sent to the countryside to perform manual labor for an indefinite period of time. [13] During the four years almost all of China's intellectuals were punished at least indirectly; half were punished by forced labor, relocation or removal from their jobs. [14]

Access to information is also a right not extended to the people of China. In view of the contents of the recent wall posters in Peking, it seems that the Chinese people know something about the Western world. But generally only very limited information is purveyed and it is selected for its propaganda value. For example, few citizens of the People's Republic knew that the United States had sent a man to the moon until Nixon visited Peking in 1972. American visitors have been astonished at questions they have heard in China, such as: "Do your old people bind their feet; can a peasant in America go to the city any time he wants; and, are cars made in the United States?" [15]

Some writers have praised the PRC for providing the Chinese masses with sufficient food and other basic necessities and employment. [16] However, it is debatable whether this could be called a "significant achievement." Economically, the ability of the PRC to feed its people may simply represent "the bare minimum achievement one could expect from any Chinese government which had enjoyed for a quarter of a century similar conditions of peace, unity, and freedom from civil war, colonialist exploitation, and external aggression—a chance no other Chinese government had had in the last hundred years." [17] A better comparison would be the change that has taken place in the rest of the world during the same period. Furthermore, the backwardness of the Chinese economy is a fact that even Peking's leaders admit. The PRC is one of the few countries in the world still using a rationing system during peace time.

In summing up, it could be said that the PRC has, by almost any standard, a poor human rights record. The new policy adopted by the Chinese Communist Party on December 25, 1978 promises to improve people's rights both in the political and civil fields and in the economic, social and cultural fields. Improvements include strengthening the social legal system, emphasis on legislative work and the independence of procurational and judicial organizations, and improving the livelihood of the people both in town and in the country. It should be noted, however, that except for the formal announcement of a halt in the campaign against the "Gang of Four" (contained in the December 25 statement), the new policy states nothing new. Similar policy lines have already been emphasized in the 11th Party Congress of August, 1977 and the 5th People's Congress of March 1978. The improvement of the human rights situation in the PRC resulting from this new policy line remains to be seen.

Human Rights in the ROC

In June 1977, Congress held hearings on the question of human rights in Taiwan, although no similar hearing has been held about the human rights situation in the PRC. The imbalance in dealing with human rights in the ROC and the PRC can be partly attributed to the fact that among intellectuals and students from Taiwan and members of the Taiwan Independence Movement in this country, most have pursued or are pursuing their advanced studies in this country; it is easy for them to invoke American standards in evaluating the human rights situation in Taiwan. It is also much easier to get information than in the case of the PRC.

The ROC's Constitution has stipulations similar to those fundamental freedoms enumerated in the Universal Human Rights Declaration. Today, the ROC government usually presents itself as a human rights respecting regime so as to win international sympathy. This can be seen from the fact that the government always defends its judgments on cases of "political crime" by asserting that human rights have been respected in the judicial process.

Political and Civil Rights

There are two major criticisms against the ROC in these areas: 1) discrimination against the native Taiwanese who constitute 85 per cent of the population in Taiwan—in particular, the absence of proportional representation and democracy; 2) the existence of martial law for three decades which undermines political and civil rights granted in the Constitution.

Does the Nationalist government discriminate against the native Taiwanese people, and, if so, in what respects? The ROC still regards itself as the government of China and therefore retains the same governmental structure it had on the Mainland. Therefore leaders and bureaucrats from China occupy most of the important seats of authority in the government. However, some degree of disproportional office-holding is a function of time. The native Taiwanese did not have any access to the Chinese civil service or military service until 1945 when Taiwan reverted to Nationalist China. Usually it takes many years to advance up the ladder in a military organization or civil bureaucracy. And this has been true of Taiwan.

Another basis for criticizing Taiwan's human rights record is the lack of general elections at the national level; these have been postponed until "Recovery of the Mainland." Thus, Taiwan is still represented as one of the thirty-five provinces of China (according to the ROC's administrative classification) in the present system of the Nationalist government. Further, the majority of the members of the parliamentary bodies were elected thirty years ago in Mainland China when the Nationalist government still controlled it. Though this situation has been somewhat improved by the supplementary elections held since 1969 under the rationale of a population increase in the Taiwan area, and by the gradual passing away of the representatives elected thirty years ago, it would probably take another decade to change the main composition of these parliamentary bodies.

On the other hand, since Chiang Ching-kuo became Premier in 1972, the situation has changed. Taiwanese have dominated Taiwan's politics at the provincial and county levels, through both elections and appointments. Now there are more and more native Taiwanese leaders moving into the decision-making level of the National government, including the newly elected Vice-President of the ROC, Hsieh Tung-ming, a native Taiwanese. Differences between political opportunities open to the Taiwanese and the Mainlanders are also rapidly disappearing. In fact, there is positive proof that, due to the efforts of the new President, young Taiwanese find government employment easier to obtain than do descendants of the Mainlanders.

Martial law remains in effect because the Nationalist government in Taiwan still regards itself as being on a wartime footing—waging an unfinished civil war against the PRC. Thus, the ROC places limits on individual freedoms and civil rights as almost all countries do during wartime. Because of the relative peace and prosperity Taiwan now enjoys, this does not seem completely justified. Yet we must not forget that Taiwan is an insecure nation facing a strong external threat. It is ninety miles from a hostile giant power which has vowed repeatedly to "liberate" Taiwan, by military means if necessary. And by Peking's own admission it sends agents—spies and saboteurs—to Taiwan. The government's worry about the threat of the PRC is now compounded by the retreat of a powerful ally, the United States, whose presence was deemed essential to Taiwan's security.

Martial law in Taiwan is not generally regarded as harsh. Few foreign visitors detect the existence of martial law because the people in Taiwan enjoy a wide variety of freedoms, and there are no curfews. It has been alleged that the government has used the enforcement of criminal laws to intimidate those who demand greater political freedoms, but the population generally supports the strict enforcement of criminal codes and swift justice. Visitors note that large cities in Taiwan are the safest in the world—allowing for a greater freedom of movement than in most other countries.

Though martial law affects the freedom of movement, the case of travel within the borders of the ROC is comparable to most Western countries. Previously the freedom of going abroad was restricted to those who had legitimate reasons such as business trips, medical care, study at the graduate level and visits to close relatives. There was considerable red tape involved in overseas travel which made the passport application time-consuming. Today, however, application procedures have been simplified under the government's *pien-min* ("to suit people's convenience") policy. More significant, the government has announced that tourism will be accepted as one of the legitimate reasons to go abroad. This new policy will make freedom of movement and residence meet the standards of most Western countries.

Freedom of religion is guaranteed in Taiwan and many regard Taiwan as a bastion of religious freedom in Asia. The only recent violation of consequence reported is the refusal to grant visas to members of Reverend Moon's Unification Church. Freedom of assembly and association is guaranteed in almost all non-political areas, while most political assemblies in Taiwan are either government-directed or government-sponsored. In this context the Chungli election riot in late 1977 deserves special notice. Though the incident was by no means a "peaceful assembly"—it involved burning a police station and several police cars—the government did not apply force to suppress the riot, and less than a dozen people who were seen setting fires during the riot were punished.

According to Burton Levin, then Director of the State Department's Office of ROC Affairs, Taiwan: "Most human rights violations have their legal basis in the martial law. Its generalized references to offenses against the security of the state and against public order and safety provide the Government ready means to act against opponents. However, the Government does not utilize all of the discretionary powers granted by that law." [18] And, while people suspected of sedition have in the past been detained without being formally charged or tried, in recent years detainees have eventually been charged and tried or released.

Though the ROC government heretofore never admitted that there were political prisoners in Taiwan, in late 1976 it disclosed that 254 persons were serving jail terms for sedition. [19] This figure seems reliable since Amnesty International has a name list of about 200 persons, of whom 95 were convicted between 1974-1976. [20] Thus, not only has there been progress in the area of human rights in Taiwan, but the government—unlike Peking —has cooperated with the United States and international organizations to allow outside criticism and suggestions for improvement.

In Taiwan, there have been only six persons sentenced to jail for sedition or related charges during the past two years. In the case of Chen Chu, former secretary to a dissident leader, the government exhibited unprecedented leniency. [21] It also deserves notice that, in the past five years, the death penalty has not been used against "political criminals," though the crime of sedition may be punished by death.

Martial law also gives the government authority to limit freedom of the press. According to Levin, the Nationalist government "conducts post-publication censorship and occasionally recalls articles of publications. It has suspended, reorganized, or banned outspoken periodicals. In recent years, the Government has allowed somewhat freer access to information about overseas developments, including events in the PRC, and it has become less restrictive in its censorship of foreign news and periodicals." [22]

Though the ruling Nationalist party owns several important newspapers, the largest two newspapers are private enterprises. However, newspapers are licensed by the government and the number of licenses has been frozen at thirty-one. Also all newspapers are limited to twelve standard pages. [23] However, these limitations on newspapers are offset by the almost unlimited freedom to publish periodicals and magazines. There are now more than 1,500 different periodicals and magazines published in Taiwan. Instead of requiring a license issued by the government, only registration with the government is required before publishing the first issue. On the other hand, in March 1978 the government announced its intention to suspend registration of new periodicals and magazines for one year because, according to the government, the existing ones were too numerous and of poor quality.

It has been reported that the real reason for suspending new registration is to prevent dissident groups from acquiring more tools for publicity. [24] This seems probable in view of the fact that in the last few years, several books and magazines (e.g., *Taiwan Political Review*) were banned because the publications were sharply criticizing the government and the ruling Nationalist Party and advocating a much more pragmatic national policy with implications of Taiwanese independence.

But we should also note that in the recent supplementary Parliamentary election campaign, some of the non-Party-owned newspapers lent an air of legitimacy to the opposition instead of the previously one-sided coverage of campaigns in favor of the Party-nominated candidates. This newfound openness was described as a "good sign" even by ranking Party officials. [25]

Economic, Social and Cultural Rights

With an annual GNP growth rate of about 10 per cent, the economic life for the people of Taiwan is generally affluent and income more equally distributed than in most countries, East or West. [26] For example: the rate of unemployment is 1.4 per cent; the rise of per capita income over the past decade, from $217 to $1,050. Regarding the equality of income distribution, the top fifth of the population earns only four times as much as the bottom fifth which is better than either the United States or Japan. [27] The average daily food intake in Taiwan is 2,800 calories and 77 grams of protein (the highest in Asia). Life expectancy has risen from 58 years in 1953 to 71 in 1978.

This material boom is also accompanied by an advance in cultural life. Since 1969, free and compulsory education has been offered through the ninth grade which makes the ROC one of the two Asian states (the other one being Japan) offering this kind of educational opportunity. A high rate of literacy, popular stress on education and multifarious cultural activities, ranging from local Taiwanese operas to Western "disco" dances, make for a full cultural life. Also, in the last few years, the government has paid special attention to housing problems of the low-income class by eliminating slum conditions in the cities and by helping people build new houses through government loans.

A Brief Comparison

After reviewing the human-rights picture on both sides of the Taiwan Strait it seems clear that individual life under Taiwan's martial law is much more free than life under Peking's "dictatorship of the proletariat." According to one observer, "despite the fact that Taiwan has an authoritarian political system, the system is not totalitarian." [28]

In Taiwan, the political order operates under a lenient martial law. There is freedom of movement, residence, and religion; partial freedom in the field of assembly, association, speech and expression; and tolerance of the existence of increasingly important dissident groups. In short, the human rights situation in the ROC is better than that in most authoritarian states. The ROC was thus classified as a "partly free" country by the 1978 Freedom House survey. On a 1-7 scale, with degree 7 being the least free, the ROC was assigned a rank of 5 on the political scale and 4 on the civil rights scale. [29]

The situation in the PRC is considerably worse. There are strong prohibitions against religion, speech and expression.

Other freedoms and rights enumerated in the UN Declaration are generally lacking in the PRC. Life under the PRC's rule is further worsened by the lack of due process of law and poverty in both material and cultural life. The political and civil rights situation in the PRC has thus been rated low in the same survey done by Freedom House. In both categories the PRC is categorized [30] as "least free" and is given a numerical rank of 6.

Human Rights Concern in the Post-Normalization Period

In normalizing relations with the PRC without questioning the human rights situation under Peking's rule, President Carter has undercut his claim that human rights enjoys priority in American foreign policy. Though normalization is a *fait accompli*, the United States cannot ignore the depressing human rights situation in the PRC. And now, lack of diplomatic relations can no longer serve as an excuse for the passive U.S. human rights policy vis-a-vis the PRC. The Carter Administration should bring human rights into the new Sino-American relations by linking improvement of human rights in the PRC with American technological and/or economic cooperation. Some might argue that this kind of linkage would upset the new relationship, yet as far as the long-term U.S.-PRC relationship is concerned, Washington may never have a better opportunity to make human rights the true soul of its China policy.

Until December 15, 1978 the ROC deserved credit for substantially cooperating with Carter's human rights campaign. It is possible that the normalization between the United States and the PRC could reduce the incentive and willingness of the Taipei government to improve human rights. The statement of Taiwan's President Chiang still emphasized the maintenance of a democratic system and the guarantee of human rights. [31] However, out of a sense of insecurity and fear of domestic instability, the government in Taipei suspended the planned parliamentary election and gave the police extended prerogatives to enforce the martial law. Persistent rumors of an impending political crackdown against the dissidents seem to have been confirmed by the January arrest of two prominent opposition figures on suspicion of sedition. [32]

More important than this, however, the people of Taiwan are now living in a state of fear that they will someday be forced to live under the control of the PRC and that their rights to freedom of speech, association, travel, residence and the ownership of property will be taken away. Further, they anticipate that families will be broken up, that property owners will become "class enemies" and that most of the population will be forced to relocate in China.

Within the present context, there is much the United States can and should do to enhance the sense of security for the government and the people in Taiwan, and thus improve the human rights situation there. President Carter has called for a renewal of the "moral" dimension of American relations abroad. On the way to this goal, we will encounter the old difficulties between moral ideals and the demands of pragmatic policy even after the normalization has been achieved.

Perhaps the most important task for the United States will be to fix a "weight" to the moral element in our cost/benefit analysis of foreign policy decisions. In calculating the balance between human rights in the PRC and in the ROC, the scales should come down solidly for guaranteeing the security of the people living in Taiwan. This will sustain an improving human rights situation already far superior to that of the mainland.

Chapter Five
TAIWAN'S OPTIONS AND
U.S. CHINA POLICY

No assessment of the consequences of U.S. recognition of the PRC would be complete without taking into account the reaction of the ROC on Taiwan. The leaders of the ROC have had to live with the possibility of derecognition for some time. Their course of action could make a considerable difference to the success or failure of U.S. policy in East Asia.

During the early 1960s, ROC leaders feared that the United States might attempt to normalize relations with the PRC. Kennedy had so much as promised this in his campaign. For that reason the ROC strongly supported Nixon for the presidency and was disappointed when he lost. During Kennedy's tenure in office, however, ROC leaders found less reason to be apprehensive of the new President than they had originally thought. Soon after he became President, Kennedy had to deal with a direct Soviet threat in Cuba and the growing Communist aggression in Southeast Asia. Thus, U.S. China policy never became a genuine concern, and Taipei made no preparations to change its policy in any important way or to reassess its dependence on the United States. It maintained its "return to the mainland" theme, a campaign in consonance with the refusal of Chiang Kai-shek and his colleagues to consider political change. The "return to the mainland" pledge also justified continued minority rule of Mainland Chinese over the Taiwanese, martial law and the circumventing of provisions in the constitution that provided for democracy and human rights. The ROC government feared internal disorder: the Taiwanese had revolted against Mainlander rule in 1947 and the Taiwanese Independence Movement was active in the United States and Japan.

During the late 1960s, as the Vietnam War expanded and the Cultural Revolution enveloped China, Taipei found a period of respite. ROC leaders contended that retaking the main-land was "70 per cent political and 30 per cent military," reflect-ing the fact that they had little confidence in conquering the PRC and hence a declining desire to make the try. During this period when opportunities, military or otherwise, presented themselves, Taipei only infrequently suggested to U.S. decision makers that direct military action be taken against the PRC. Little was said in response to American scholars as well as Congressmen and others who suggested a two-Chinas policy, as long as it did not include an immediate Taiwanese rule; the Nationalist Chinese rulers were resigned to the fact that they were not going back to the mainland and that their future lay in Taiwan.

Growing cooperation between Mainlander Chinese and Taiwanese also became apparent. This was particularly evident in the late 1960s and early 1970s when Chiang Ching-kuo used his authority to put more Taiwanese into positions of impor-tance. [1]

When Richard Nixon became President in 1969, ROC leaders believed that it would be some time before Peking would end its self-imposed isolationism and try to join the world com-munity at Taipei's expense. They reckoned without a proper assessment of the Sino-Soviet dispute or the inclinations of Nixon himself. ROC leaders were therefore both surprised and upset with the Nixon visit to Peking and the Shanghai Communique that concluded his journey. The Communique abruptly ended American evolution toward a two-Chinas policy—stating instead what was Nationalist China's own official belief in one China on both sides of the Taiwan Straits. The United States also promised to withdraw its forces from Taiwan in the context of talks with Peking. These reverses were mitigated somewhat by the Com-munique's ambiguities: normalization was not defined, nor was there a timetable. This left the ROC some room for maneuver and gave an opportunity to attempt to influence public opinion in the United States as well as in Congress. Finally, Nixon clearly promised to guarantee the ROC's security.

During the Ford Administration, though White House leaders continued to cite the Shanghai Communique as the basis of U.S. China policy, U.S. investments in Taiwan increased, weapons were sold to Taiwan and U.S. weapons manufacturers were allowed to set up factories on the island. This activity reassured the Nationalists. [2] Meanwhile, U.S. leaders expressed some concern that Peking had failed to live up to the provisions in the Shanghai Communique: U.S. news reporters were not given meaningful opportunities to operate in the PRC; U.S.-PRC trade, after initially increasing, dropped; and cultural and other exchanges did not develop to any meaningful degree. Nor was normalization concretely defined by President Ford. Therefore, to ROC leaders, U.S. China policy was not to be interpreted to mean that the United States would accept the PRC's conditions for recognition—leaving Taiwan with the hope of eventual self-determination and self-rule.

When Jimmy Carter became President, Nationalist Chinese leaders had cause for optimism. Carter had promised unequivocally during the campaign that he would not "sacrifice or abandon Taiwan." This must be seen against Ford's earlier statement that he would seek "full normalization"—apparently meaning formal diplomatic relations. And Carter's support for the ROC continued after Carter became President. In May 1977, at a press conference, President Carter made the following points regarding China policy: 1) while the Shanghai Communique stated that there was only one China, it did not say who the representative of China was; 2) there was no timetable or deadline in normalization of relations with Peking; and 3) the United States was unwilling to see the people of Taiwan pressured or attacked by the Mainland. [3]

Second, Carter initially took a harder line toward Communist nations by pressing the human rights campaign. This policy direction, interpreted by Taipei to mean a return to a foreign policy based on ideology and moral principles (and anti-Communism), suggested that Carter might reverse the process of normalization—even though he had stated that U.S. China policy would be founded upon the provisions of the Shanghai Communique. The Nationalist Chinese, cognizant of the PRC's human rights record, believed this to be another barrier against Carter's preference for the PRC.

Third, Carter promised a foreign policy based on open diplomacy and a departure from power politics, balance of power and secret negotiations, characteristic, in his view, of the previous administration. Carter also promised consensus—meaning that Congress and the American people would be consulted in foreign policy decisions and that their views would be taken into consideration on all important matters.

This third point was especially significant because the ROC was making a constant effort to influence public opinion in the United States and kept close watch on American public opinion polls and the mood of Congress. Although American public opinion toward the PRC became more "positive" after Nixon's visit in 1972, it did not reach fifty per cent in the ensuing years and after 1975 dropped markedly—to 28 per cent that year. [4] In following years it dropped even further. Meanwhile, the U.S. public's attitude toward the ROC was consistently over the fifty per cent mark and showed increases in 1976 and 1977, probably reflecting a reaction to Peking's three conditions for normalization. When asked about the future of Taiwan, pollsters consistently registered more than a two-thirds majority favoring policies leading to Taiwan's independence—and this figure was increasing. [5] A poll conducted by the Foreign Policy Association in 1976 indicated that the American public felt that the eventual independence of Taiwan was preferable to any other policy. [6] Asked whether the United States should break diplomatic ties with the ROC, 53 per cent responded no, while most polls up to that time favored breaking diplomatic ties though not all ties. [7] In July 1978, a Harris-ABC News Service poll recorded that, by a margin of 66 to 19 per cent, the American people opposed derecognition of the ROC and by a 64 to 19 per cent margin wanted the United States to maintain the defense pact with the ROC. [8]

This view was not limited to public opinion. In July 1977 a group of university scholars did a survey of mass media and political leaders and ascertained a high interest in China policy as compared to other foreign policy issues. [9] The survey also revealed that more than 90 per cent of this group were against accepting Peking's three conditions for normalization and this was true of Republicans, Democrats and independents alike. This same group also replied that they did not feel (by a majority of 67 per cent) that the ROC could withstand Peking's pressures if the United States disengaged from Taiwan. Seventy-two per cent felt that U.S. world leadership and credibility in Asia would be hurt by not making the proper provisions for Taiwan during the course of normalization, and by a margin of 45 to 26 per cent, it was felt that Taipei might take "drastic action" if the United States withdrew. By a three-to-one margin this group also favored U.S. recognition of an independent Taiwan, if Taipei decided to declare its independence. Only 5 per cent favored accepting Peking's three conditions, while a majority blamed the conditions for a lack of progress in U.S.-PRC normalization. Finally, most favored not altering relations with the ROC as a minimum position in negotiating with Peking.

Most of the newspapers in the United States also supported Taiwan's independence and self-determination, as did the U.S. Congress. [10] Both the *New York Times* and the *Washington Post* had published editorials opposing the dumping of Taiwan. Polls taken in Congress in mid-1978—less than six months before Carter made the announcement that the United States would grant diplomatic recognition to the PRC and acknowledged that Taiwan is part of China—showed only six members of the House of Representatives favoring accepting Peking's three conditions. [11] In June, the Senate passed a resolution, by a vote of 94 to 0, stating that the President should consult the Senate before abrogating a treaty, with specific reference to the U.S.-ROC Defense Pact. In October, two months prior to Carter's move, a poll was taken which showed fifty-three Senators opposed to severing relations with the ROC and only three in favor of accepting Peking's conditions. [12]

It is difficult to know how much influence the ROC had

on public opinion in the United States. The efforts that Taipei made in improving its human rights record, upgrading democracy in Taiwan and in giving Taiwanese more opportunities to participate in government did have a positive affect in the United States. So did their efforts to attract U.S. tourists and allow them to see whatever they wanted in Taiwan—in contrast to the restrictions placed on travelers in the PRC. Taipei did seek to influence public opinion in the United States through friends who wrote letters to the editors of important papers and by financing visits by Congressmen and their staffs to Taiwan. The appeal was low-keyed, stressing ROC improvements in the context of a U.S. concern for human rights and the right of the people of Taiwan to determine their future.

The Nationalist Chinese were shocked when Carter acted in a manner quite reminiscent of his "power political" predecessors, overriding in a secret and surprising way the apparent preference of public opinion and the mood of Congress. The White House notified the ROC only seven hours before the President's impending recognition of the PRC, further undermining the esteem of the leadership. The Nationalist Chinese felt deceived and betrayed.

The ROC government now regards the foreign policy of the Carter Administration as dangerously unpredictable. Nationalist Chinese leaders, and the populace of Taiwan, also have cause to distrust the U.S. promise of weapons sales, which was perhaps the major solace they had in the U.S.-PRC agreement. The Carter Administration has been unclear on its weapons sales policy. It belatedly concluded that it had promised Peking not to make new commitments to sell military equipment to Taiwan during 1979 while the mutual U.S.-ROC Defense Treaty remains in effect. Carter promised continued U.S. weapons sales to Taiwan even though in July 1978 he refused the sale of sixty F-4 jet aircraft. In late 1978 the Carter Administration also turned down the sale of F-5 aircraft. ROC leaders certainly have reason to anticipate that Peking will strongly reiterate its objections concerning the sale of U.S. weapons to Taiwan. Finally, Taiwan cannot help but conclude that Peking has been flexible on the Taiwan issue only when it has perceived that it has something to gain from the United States. [13]

The pressure Peking can mount on Taiwan runs the gamut from threatening invasion, attempting infiltration and undermining the island's economy. [14] The PRC may be able to pressure foreign businessmen to withdraw from Taiwan. Threats can create an environment of insecurity so that investors and those foreigners doing business in Taiwan pull out. Similarly the PRC can dump goods on the world market similar or identical to those produced in Taiwan. Any of these actions would have a tremendous impact on Taiwan's economy and could be countered only with outside help.

In short, while the Nationalists do not perceive any immediate or pending danger as a result of Carter's moves, they have little grounds for optimism about their future. The ROC's mood has undoubtedly changed from one of trust and reliance to one of independence and challenge. Their concern is primarily one of survival.

With this in mind it is instructive to assess what their options might be and their ramifications for the United States and to the rest of the world, as well. Taiwan's apparent options are 1) a declaration of independence, 2) a deal or alliance with the Soviet Union, 3) construction of nuclear weapons, and 4) any two or all of these. These options all present obvious problems and dangers to U.S. interests in Asia and to American relations with other Asian powers.

The Independence Option

The first and perhaps the most likely move that Taipei could make would be to declare its independence of China, repudiate the claim that Taiwan is part of China, and perhaps change its name—to, say, the Taiwan Republic. This would certainly appeal to the native Taiwanese, though it would mean a profound break with the ideology of the Nationalist Chinese government. Such action would be encouraged 1) if the PRC presses for a reversion of the island to its control and the Nationalist Chinese find the United States reluctant to supply sufficient arms, or 2) if the PRC is regarded as too weak and dependent on U.S. or Japanese favor to make effective protest.

The implications of independence would be numerous. Taipei would probably evacuate the off-shore islands where one-third of its soldiers are stationed and thus sever all ties with the mainland. At an appropriate time in the future, it could also invite officials from the United Nations, or simply some known and trusted world leaders, to supervise a plebiscite on Taiwan—which would surely reflect an overwhelming majority in favor of independence. [15] At the same time, Taipei might apply for membership in the United Nations. It could also change its name in world organizations where it already has membership and apply to others where it may be able to get membership. The new "Taiwan Republic" might ask all investors to renegotiate their loans and business operations in Taiwan, recognizing the independent status of the country. It could do the same with airlines that want to use Taiwan's airspace and ships that use the Taiwan Strait. In such case it would ask for recognition as an independent governing authority, indicating that it is not simply a part of China.

Taiwan's "Moscow Card"

A second option for Taiwan is to seek closer relations with the Soviet Union, in three possible scenarios: 1) an understanding that if the PRC builds up forces in Fukien Province adjacent to Taiwan in preparation for an invasion, the Kremlin will increase tension on the Sino-Soviet border; 2) allowing the Soviet Navy and Air Force the use of bases in Taiwan; 3) signing a formal alliance with the Soviet Union.

The first step—a secret agreement with Moscow to offset any PRC troop build-up in preparation for an invasion—can be done without endangering Taiwan's ties with the West or any other harmful repercussions. Taipei could be expected to take the next steps according to its perception of the seriousness of the threat of PRC invasion or other forms of pressure.

Since the mid-1960s, when Sino-Soviet relations took another major step backwards as a result of the rhetoric of the Great Proletarian Cultural Revolution, there have been various hints that Soviet leaders do not favor Taiwan's incorporation by the PRC. In 1965, pictures of the ROC flag were first published in the Soviet Union—which, in Peking's view, constituted recognition of the ROC as a separate country. In 1966, a Soviet magazine referred to Taiwan as a "state" and the following year this was repeated by TASS, the official Soviet news agency. [16] In 1970, the Soviet press, at the time Vice-President Agnew was touring Asia, referred to Taiwan as a "country." [17] In 1968, Victor Louis, commonly regarded as an unofficial representative of the Soviet government, visited Taiwan and talked with Chiang Ching-kuo— then Defense Minister. The PRC has claimed that other trips followed, although evidence is lacking. [18] In 1967, Moscow's representative to the UN hinted to the world body a two-Chinas solution to the China representation question. [19]

There is also some evidence that the mutual interests of the Soviet Union and the ROC have already included a military dimension. In 1969, when the Soviet Union demanded that the PRC initiate border talks and received no response, ROC paramilitary forces raided a military base in Fukien across the Taiwan Strait. [20] The PRC's defense plan announced shortly thereafter indicated that in the event of a further escalation of Sino-Soviet hostilities, it anticipated a two-pronged invasion: from the north and from the Taiwan area. Peking at the same time accused the ROC of holding discussions with Soviet Union officials in Tokyo concerning mutual defense interests. In May 1973—just two days before David Bruce went to Peking to head the American "liaison office"—two Soviet warships passed through the Taiwan Strait and circumnavigated Taiwan. This was the first occasion since World War II that Soviet naval vessels had gone through the Strait.

Taiwanese attitudes toward the Soviet Union have been changing subtly. In the 1960s, Taiwan's press began to discriminate between Soviet and Chinese Communism. In 1969, not long after Victor Louis visited Taiwan, a former ROC Deputy Minister of Education went to the Soviet Union as did a number of members of the ROC delegation to the World Tourism Conference held in Bulgaria. [21] On a number of occasions there were reports that Taiwan planned to allow the Soviet Union use of base facilities or in fact lease them a base in Taiwan or the Pescadores if the United States moved its embassy to Peking. In all cases, the reports were subsequently denied officially in Taipei, but owing to the number of the reports and credibility of the sources, it seems certain that they did emanate from the ROC. The most recent of such reports came from a Greek newspaper editor who visited Taiwan in August 1978. [22]

In 1971, when the ROC was expelled from the United Nations, Foreign Minister Chow Shu-kai announced that Taiwan planned to trade with the Soviet Union (Taiwan-made products were subsequently seen in Moscow and other Soviet cities by tourists) and that he envisioned secret talks between Taiwan and the Soviet Union similar to U.S.-PRC talks in Warsaw. [23] He went on to say that if the United States makes important concessions to Peking, or seeks to completely disengage from the Western Pacific, then "the free nations of Asia would begin turning toward the Soviet Union." In April 1978, according to Peking, secret talks between Moscow and Taipei were going on in Vienna, and in July Peking reported "collusion" between the Soviet Union and the ROC. [24]

Clearly it has been in Taiwan's interest for some time to maintain some contact with the Soviet Union based on mutual interests and a common enemy. This was even more true after 1971, when Taipei had good reason to question its relationship with the United States. Since the Carter Administration granted formal diplomatic recognition to Peking, Taipei has had even better cause to seek ties with Moscow. There is little doubt that if Taipei perceives a PRC military build-up or even economic and political pressure on Taiwan to force Taipei to negotiate an incorporation, Chiang will seek some understanding with the Soviet Union in any form that seems appropriate.

The Nuclear Choice

Taiwan's third option is to build nuclear weapons. The ROC has signed the Nuclear Nonproliferation Treaty and has made other promises not to build nuclear weapons. Nonetheless, there is reason to believe that Taiwan can and might do so as circumstances change.

The ROC is a state with a worsening security situation, has outcast or "pariah" diplomatic status, and has little hope of matching the conventional military power of its adversary. These are classic reasons for considering the nuclear option. The deterrence provided by such a weapon becomes more attractive as the only way to "equalize" the military situation, while calling attention to Taiwan's right to exist as the seventh nuclear power.

Taiwan has the capability to produce atomic weapons. ROC scientists have been doing research on nuclear energy since the 1950s and in 1961 built a small reactor to enlarge their knowledge and expertise. [25] To date, more than a thousand ROC nuclear physicists have received training in the United States and have returned to Taiwan. [26] The ROC has purchased U.S. and Canadian equipment for both the generation of electricity and research. Currently Taiwan has six reactors that are to be used for electricity generation; the first was put into operation in 1977. [27] When all are working, they will provide Taiwan with over 40 per cent of its electricity. The reactors' byproducts can be used to produce a fairly large stockpile of bombs if diverted to that use.

One of Taiwan's research reactors was purchased from Canada not long before Ottawa granted diplomatic recognition to Peking, leaving the Canadians without control over fuel used in the reactor. This reactor was an improved version of the one

Canada sold to India; the latter was instrumental in the manufacture of the nuclear device India exploded in the Rajasthan Desert in 1974. In addition, Taiwan commenced construction of a reprocessing laboratory in 1970; it was completed more than two years ago. [28] In 1976 it was reported that the ROC was secretly reprocessing nuclear fuel. [29]

It is unlikely that a delivery system will present a serious problem. Both the F5 and F4 fighter aircraft possessed by Taiwan can be fitted with nuclear weapons; some of the F4 fighter planes the United States had stationed in Taiwan are equipped to carry atomic bombs. The ROC may also be able to send atomic weapons by missile. In 1976, fifteen ROC engineers were at M.I.T. learning the sophisticated technology required to build internal navigation systems, in other words, the techniques for guiding nuclear-tipped missiles. After ROC opponents discovered what the fifteen were doing and publicized their mission, the State Department cancelled their visas and sent them back to Taiwan. [30] In 1977, Taiwan reportedly purchased Gabriel surface-to-surface missiles from Israel along with Israeli technical assistance for installing them on Nationalist Chinese destroyers. [31] In October 1978, the ROC National Day celebrations included home-produced missiles. [32] Taiwan now has the third-largest military budget in East Asia, after the PRC and Japan, and spends by far the largest percentage on highly sophisticated weaponry.

Will Taiwan go nuclear? This, of course, depends upon how it perceives U.S. promises and the potential threat from the PRC. Some facts concerning its view toward restraints or limitations are instructive. In 1968 the ROC signed the Nuclear Nonproliferation Treaty and, in 1970, gave its formal ratification. According to this treaty, the ROC foreswore the development of nuclear weapons, but in turn was guaranteed protection from the threat or use of threat by a nuclear power. Both the United States and the Soviet Union guaranteed this. At the time of signing, several ROC officials said the treaty did not mean that Taiwan could not build nuclear weapons—since Taiwan is China and China already is a nuclear power. Although such an interpretation was not generally accepted, it may become more persuasive among ranking ROC leaders inasmuch as the United States has stated there is but one China and President Carter has said that Taiwan is a part of China.

When Taipei ratified the Nonproliferation Treaty it also agreed to International Atomic Energy Agency (IAEA) inspections of its nuclear power plants. This is supposed to insure that spent fuel is not diverted to use for weapons and to prevent reprocessing to produce plutonium. Taipei has continued to abide by IAEA guidelines and to allow the IAEA to carry out inspections. This was subsequently done under U.S. aegis. Agreements between the United States and the ROC, however, include only U.S.-supplied hardware and fuel. Thus there would be no provision for inspection of a significant quantity of fuel that Taiwan has purchased from South Africa—with whom Taiwan has recently upgraded its diplomatic contacts.

The ROC evidently has both the facilities and the capability to make nuclear weapons. At the same time, ROC leaders have flatly denied any intention of building nuclear weapons. When asked about going nuclear they have often replied that nuclear weapons are not as useful as the U.S.-ROC Defense Pact.

Taipei is certainly in a position to bargain with the United States and the world community to the effect that it will not divert its nuclear fuels into the production of weapons as long as there are IAEA and U.S. inspectors in Taiwan. Taipei could also follow Israel's example and promote conjecture or speculation about Taiwan's possession of nuclear weapons. This may have more impact than actually becoming a nuclear power. Or, Taipei could publicly announce that it has developed nuclear capabilities but has not chosen to build a bomb—and that it will do so only in the event of a build-up of forces across the Taiwan Strait. A nation can complete all of the measures needed to build nuclear weapons without taking the final step.

Taiwan's Options and U.S. China Policy

Each of the options presented above—independence, a

Soviet alliance, nuclear proliferation—presents major problems for the future of U.S.-PRC relations and the stability of East Asian politics. The PRC would regard an independent Taiwan as a rebellious province, made all the more dangerous by the possibility of Soviet alliance or proliferation. The United States, having agreed already that Taiwan is part of China, might then find itself caught between public opinion highly favorable to Taiwanese survival and a violent Chinese attempt to recover the "province." The Taiwan issue would no longer be a matter of subsiding interest to U.S.-PRC relations.

A Taiwan-Soviet relationship poses even greater difficulties for the United States and the PRC. It would place Soviet power in a critical waterway while signaling local allies and friends of the United States and the PRC that the Soviet Union was the real arbiter of the destiny of small states in the region. The United States would stand condemned in Peking (and Tokyo) as a strategic blunderer; Peking would stand condemned as impotent in the face of Soviet deterrence.

The nuclear option can hardly have a beneficial impact on U.S. interests either. If Taiwan succeeds in strengthening its bargaining powers as a legitimate, independent entity through nuclear proliferation, the U.S. policy to discourage such acts will have suffered a devastating blow. In a region so unstable as the Far East, with the local states anxious over their security in the wake of recent change and superpower rivalries, the Taiwan example may become contagious. Korea and even Japan would be strongly influenced by the Taiwan experience. The United States would be blamed for driving Taiwan to proliferate and then failing to prevent proliferation.

The only safe course of action to prevent these dangers would seem to be a strong and sustaining defense tie between the United States and Taiwan. Such a connection, of course, gives the island the wherewithal to resist incorporation by the mainland. But both Washington and Peking may have to accept this paradox if greater dangers to their mutual interests are to be avoided.

Chapter Six
THE UNITED STATES AND
THE FUTURE OF TAIWAN

If anything has emerged from this examination of American policy toward China, it is that recognition of Peking carries in its wake far-reaching consequences: strategic, economic, legal and moral. These consequences and the reaction to them will determine the success or failure of the "triangular" strategy Washington now practices amid the rivalry between Moscow and Peking. Moreover, the fate of Taiwan is far from settled, and the choices for the Republic of China are still highly important to U.S. security interests.

In strategic terms America's China policy seems to run serious risks of proportion and timing. First, as an informal ally, the PRC expects the United States to alleviate, if not eliminate, the Soviet threat against China. In part, this means the improvement of America's own military posture. Given the PRC's own weak military forces, however, as the United States finally begins to alter the Soviet-American balance in its favor, Washington's need for Peking will diminish. On the other hand, if Peking wishes the United States to "hold off" the Soviets while the PRC, with liberal Western technological assistance, strengthens its military position, then Washington will harden its current position toward Moscow for the sake of Peking's long-term interests.

There is little reason to believe that the Sino-Soviet dispute will abate. U.S. policy therefore enjoys a certain "cushion of hostility," giving Washington some appeal to both Moscow and Peking. It would be unwise to conclude that if the United States deliberately offered incentives to one side or the other their dispute would be resolved.

Another problem arises from the assumption that the United States can achieve a four-power balance in Asia. First, in simple structural terms it is difficult to see how such a balance of power can create stability over a long period. A four-power balance assumes that the United States can pursue an alliance policy with China and Japan in order to restrain the Soviet Union. For a century the United States has consistently been unable to maintain friendly relations—let alone alliances—with both at the same time. Despite the Treaty of Peace and Friendship between Japan and China, serious issues divide them, including competition in Southeast Asia, a territorial dispute, and their relations with Taiwan and Korea.

The fate of detente with the Soviet Union is also at issue. The United States has tried to alleviate Soviet concerns, though clearly intending recognition of Peking to be a signal of sorts cautioning against Soviet ambitions. But the Carter Administration did not manage this delicate maneuver very well. On the eve of Carter's announcement, the President's National Security Adviser, Zbigniew Brzezinski, called in Soviet Ambassador Anatoly Dobrynin to tell him of the decision, and to ask him to convey to Mr. Brezhnev the assurance that the United States' action was not directed against the Russians. A few days later, Brezhnev responded with a personal message, which Carter labeled "very positive in tone." Specially, he mentioned Brezhnev's understanding that "our commitment is to peace in the entire world," acknowledging the fact that our new relationship with the People's Republic of China "will contribute to world peace."

On December 21, the Soviet news agency challenged President Carter's interpretation, pointing out that Brezhnev's response included a negative side: "The message draws attention to the fact that the joint American-Chinese communique contains expressions whose direction is beyond doubt, if one bears in mind the usual vocabulary of the Chinese leaders." The Soviets were displeased with the inclusion of the word "hegemony" (Peking's code word for Soviet imperialism) in the joint U.S.-PRC communique of December 15.

The Soviets were soon to demonstrate their displeasure with the budding friendship between Peking and Washington.

Within less than a month after President Carter's recognition of Peking, Soviet-backed Vietnamese "liberators" captured the Cambodian capital of Phnom Penh. Representatives of the People's Republic of China, America's new diplomatic partner in Asia, escaped across the Cambodian border into Thailand. Initially, the PRC was unable to aid her Cambodian ally, and the U.S. gave diplomatic support to Peking when the matter was raised in the UN Security Council. Within a few weeks, however, after the PRC began punishing Vietnam by launching an invasion across the border separating the two countries, Washington displayed an aloof diplomacy toward Peking. Moscow immediately pledged that the Soviet Union would "honor its obligations to Vietnam," without revealing what action would be taken. After capturing Lang Son, a key communications center in northern Vietnam, the Chinese appeared to have "punished" Vietnam sufficiently and announced their intention to withdraw. Moscow reinforced Vietnam but did not engage its own forces. Both the PRC and Vietnam claimed a victory.

On the strategic side, America's policy toward China still suffers from the same ambiguities as before recognition. It is not clear how Washington and Peking are to "divide the labor" of containing the Soviets. Likewise, it is not evident how far this process can go without upsetting Soviet-American detente. And, above all, as the Cambodian episode made clear, the potency of the anti-Soviet forces in Asia remains to be demonstrated. Given Peking's military weakness and Washington's military reluctance, this is the most immediate problem besetting the new constellation of forces in Asia.

While the benefits accruing to the United States from its recognition of the PRC remain speculative, some of the costs are more concrete. In the Far East, American credibility had been shaken badly by recent events, ranging from the Vietnam disaster to a further decline of the falling dollar. Though the Asian states were aware that normalization was necessary and inevitable, they were shocked by its timing and the terms Washington accepted.

The official "welcome" to the news of U.S.-PRC normalization extended by those East Asian countries is one thing, and the American credibility in the minds of their leaders is quite another. Even when expressing their affirmative attitude toward normalization most of those countries gave guarded approval.

U.S. China policy was partially built upon commercial gains which appear, to a large extent, to rest on false hopes. Three points deserve repeating here. First, ties with China for reasons of business and profit contradict America's human rights policy, or at least detract from it; the same is true of the strategic rationale for the U.S. move. Second, there is little hope that the United States will be able to gain as much from the China trade as it may sacrifice in trade and investment in Taiwan. It will be some years, assuming continued good relations between the United States and the People's Republic of China, before trade with the PRC equals U.S.-ROC trade. It will be even longer before U.S. investment in China exceeds its investment in Taiwan. Third—a point that should be underscored—U.S. business profits depend upon the trading partner having the capital to buy American products. Taiwan does; China does not.

It is also important to realize that China's shopping list from the United States may endanger American security interests—not to mention our relations with the Soviet Union. It is certainly not wise to sell China offensive weapons and weapons systems or related technology that can be used against either the Soviet Union or any of China's neighbors, most of whom are U.S. allies. Other things which China might purchase from American businessmen it can purchase elsewhere and will only buy from America for political reasons. Peking may in the future try to use American businessmen to influence U.S. foreign policy. There is also considerable evidence that the PRC has concluded too many trade deals with other countries; Peking has tried to expand its trade more rapidly than it can manage. Thus, there may be little left for American businessmen even predicating a friendly atmosphere.

The legal consequences of Carter's act of recognition will be very complex, especially for future U.S. relations with

Taiwan. Except for the offshore islands of Quemoy and Matsu, the PRC has no legal basis to claim any territory under the jurisdiction of the Republic of China. A new U.S. China policy cannot change this legal reality, even if the official U.S. attitude toward Taiwan's legal status remains ambiguous. Roger Sullivan, Deputy Assistant Secretary of State for East Asian and Pacific Affairs and a ranking member of the Christopher Mission to Taiwan, pointed out in Taipei that when the U.S. "acknowledged the Chinese position that there is but one China and Taiwan is part of China" in the joint communique with Peking, it did not recognize the PRC's claim over Taiwan because the word "Chinese" meant the Chinese people on both sides of the Strait. [1] For centuries China has been divided just as Europe has been, and several times there has been more than one China or Sinofied region. At present, there are two or more Chinas—four if we include Singapore, which is a sovereign nation-state and will probably never be incorporated by China, and Hong Kong, which has had colonial status for more than a hundred years. Although clearly larger than the other two Chinas, Taiwan falls between them in terms of the proportion of its population which is Chinese, its historical ties to China and its proximity to China. On the other hand, trends in Taiwan's culture and in its population's desires and views of the future suggest that Taiwan should remain independent, a separate nation-state called the Republic of China or Taiwan. Changes in international law and the world culture would also suggest this. Yet, the most influential actor with regard to Taiwan's future—the United States—recently changed its position when the U.S. President acknowledged that Taiwan is part of China.

The reality of two separate Chinas, however, has not gone away. Even if Taiwan is considered a "disputed" territory, it should be handled according to the prevalent international practice since World War II: the wishes of the inhabitants must be considered. This would reflect a nearly unanimous decision not to become a part of China, nor to accept an autonomous status or a vague relationship with Peking—in short, not to accept anything short of complete and sovereign autonomy.

In the meantime, other ties will apparently be maintained with Taiwan as if it were a sovereign nation-state. These will include commercial, cultural and a host of other treaties and agreements. Continued tourist traffic from the United States and other countries entering Taiwan, business transactions and other contacts will also follow the pattern of state-to-state interaction. In short, we and the rest of the world will continue to act in most ways as if Taiwan were a sovereign nation.

Apparently President Carter did not take human rights into consideration when pursuing normalization with the PRC. This has already weakened the President's own avowal that human rights is the "soul of American foreign policy" by revealing the contradiction between moral ideals and realpolitik. In the wake of recognition, the United States should begin to press Peking on human rights if the Administration's human rights campaign is to be taken seriously in the future.

Also, the human rights situation in the ROC has been damaged as a result of the new U.S. China policy: e.g., the supplementary Parliamentary election was suspended immediately after Carter's announcement on December 15, 1978. With a national sense of unity in the wake of American derecognition, the government might choose to ignore both the opinions of the dissidents and the advice of the liberals. Worse than that, the conservatives among the Chinese Nationalists might press the government to be less tolerant of dissident groups. A Congressional resolution to guarantee the security of Taiwan would help stabilize the human rights situation in the ROC.

Finally, there is the problem of Taiwan's reaction to a new China policy. Taipei did not expect the United States to recognize the People's Republic of China on the PRC's terms, which included derecognition of the Republic of China, eventual termination of the defense pact, and American acknowledgment that Taiwan is part of China. ROC chagrin was reflected in the public reaction of President Chiang Ching-kuo: "During the period between Nixon's 1972 visit to the Mainland and the U.S. announcement of its intention to establish diplomatic relations with the Chinese communist regime, the U.S. declared at least 20 times that it would maintain friendship and diplomatic relations with the Republic of China and honor the mutual defense treaty. The U.S. also said it would not discuss another country's destiny behind its back." [2]

Though not in any immediate danger, Taiwan will soon be faced with critical choices for the future. ROC leaders may decide to declare independence, to ally with the Soviet Union, to "go nuclear," or to adopt two or three of these options. Any of these decisions would create serious problems for Washington and Peking. Any combination of them might destabilize East Asian strategic relations and possibly even international politics.

Some skeptics argue that such moves would entail great risks for Taiwan. But if absorption by the PRC is the alternative, the risks may well be taken. Taiwan has already embarked in a certain direction by refusing to negotiate with Peking and by rebuffing Peking's friendly overtures in the wake of American derecognition. [3] The option of an alliance with the Soviet Union or of building nuclear weapons could be accomplished in secret in order to avoid undesirable ramifications. Thus, the exercise of either option by ROC leaders could remain unknown or uncertain until Taiwan were seriously threatened, at which time a crisis situation would result for all parties involved.

The analysis of U.S. China policy made here can be concluded by saying that our policy now needs moderation and should be conducted with less flamboyance and more caution. The decision to grant diplomatic recognition to the PRC, and to derecognize Taipei while acknowledging that Taiwan is part of China, was clearly based upon inadequate analysis of the consequences.

Toward a New Peking

Perhaps we can find a way out of our self-imposed problems once we realize that the U.S. China policy has been predicated upon some exaggerated views of China, particularly with regard to the PRC's ability to offset the growing military power of the Soviet Union. A partial remedy may come through an awareness that China is not a superpower and that it will not become one in the near future, if ever, even with American help and despite wishful thinking on the part of some American decision-makers.

We should be aware that not all the tensions have gone out of U.S.-PRC relations. The change in relations has been rather abrupt and has been founded upon the decisions of leaders without mass support on either side. In short, a former enemy has suddenly become a close friend. Hence, caution should be exercised lest there occur serious disappointment and a regression to earlier, unfriendly relations. In this connection, it should also be mentioned that it is uncertain, even from official policy pronouncements, how Chinese officials perceive the United States or what exactly they expect from the recent change in relations with America. China still criticizes the superpowers and the imperialists, though the Soviet Union is attacked more bitterly than the United States.

Another reason to advise caution and less expectation in U.S.-China relations is the evolution of U.S. relations with the Soviet Union. The survival of the United States depends upon rational thinking prevailing in U.S.-Soviet relations. Hence it is unwise to try to use China against the Soviet Union, both in view of America's relationship with the Soviet Union and Moscow's fear of China. Playing the China card could be dangerous to U.S.-Soviet stability.

The Taiwan issue is also far from resolved. If the United States continues to supply Taiwan with weapons, Taiwan will never, at least in the foreseeable future, be a part of China—as President Carter has acknowledged. The people of Taiwan will use American weapons if they continue to have access to them, will maintain their independence from the People's Republic and will not negotiate with Peking. If Peking continues to regard Taiwan as a part of China, as it apparently does, at some point in the future this contradiction may result in a crisis.

Finally, it should be underscored that U.S. recognition

of the PRC in December 1978 was done in terms contrary to the inclination of Congress and American public opinion. This reduces the possibility of consensus and public support for U.S.-PRC relations. Clearly, U.S. China policy needs the support of the Congress and the American people. U.S.-PRC friendship needs to be founded upon a platform of trust and good feelings. Furthermore, China policy may become a partisan issue, Democrats and Republicans taking opposing views, and may lead to a different kind of relationship with China, depending upon which party is in control of the White House or the Congress. Major disagreements on China policy have occurred in the past. In recent years, leaders of both parties have worked together to formulate a workable China policy and this remains true today. However, one of the consequences of Carter's China policy appears to be an undermining of this bipartisanship.

The Carter Administration is planning to create a new entity (called the American Institute in Taiwan), through which the United States would maintain its cultural, economic and military links to Taiwan. On March 13, both houses of Congress approved legislation giving the Carter Administration the essential mechanism it sought to maintain unofficial ties with Taiwan while giving diplomatic recognition to China. On February 15, bowing to tremendous U.S. pressure, the Republic of China set up an organization called the "Coordination Council for North American Affairs" to handle its side of U.S.-Taiwan relations. The Council will have its headquarters in Taipei and its main office in Washington, and there will be branches in New York, San Francisco, Chicago, Los Angeles, Honolulu, Seattle, Houston and Atlanta. According to an ROC spokesman, U.S.-Taiwan relations "will have the qualities of officiality."

Some members of Congress urged that the mechanisms established both by the United States and Taiwan be given official status. If it was possible to maintain a diplomatic liaison office in Peking prior to diplomatic recognition of that country, it should have been possible to maintain such an office in Taipei, despite the withdrawal of official diplomatic recognition of the

Republic of China. Representatives of the ROC should enjoy the same diplomatic privileges, rights and courtesies they enjoyed prior to the U.S. recognition of the People's Republic. U.S. representatives on Taiwan should enjoy a comparable status.

During the debate in both houses over the Taiwan legislation, it became clear that many lawmakers wanted to change relations with Taiwan as little as possible. Relatively few Senators and Representatives opposed President Carter's decision to recognize Peking, but many were unwilling to weaken economic and military bonds with Taiwan. Because of Congressional regard for an old ally, and despite the myth of "one China," the United States will be dealing with the reality of two Chinas.

Over the last hundred years, U.S.-China relations have alternated between close, friendly ties and antipathy or bitterness. These cycles were the result of too much enthusiasm and exaggerated expectations by both sides. Both the United States and the PRC are too important to world peace to risk repeating the cycle. But a realistic basis for relations certainly does not include the sacrifice of Taiwan. America has principles, and only by remaining true to those principles can the United States be a useful friend of the PRC. The United States must sustain its pledge that "normalization will not jeopardize the well-being of the people of Taiwan."

Appendix A
MUTUAL DEFENSE TREATY BETWEEN THE UNITED STATES AND THE REPUBLIC OF CHINA (1954)

The Parties to this Treaty,

Reaffirming their faith in the purposes and principles of the Charter of the United Nations and their desire to live in peace with all peoples and all Governments, and desiring to strengthen the fabric of peace in the West Pacific Area,

Recalling with mutual pride the relationship which brought their two peoples together in a common bond of sympathy and mutual ideals to fight side by side against imperialist aggression during the last war,

Desiring to declare publicly and formally their sense of unity and their common determination to defend themselves against external armed attack, so that no potential aggressor could be under the illusion that either of them stands alone in the West Pacific Area, and

Desiring further to strengthen their present efforts for collective defense for the preservation of peace and security pending the development of a more comprehensive system of regional security in the West Pacific Area,

Have agreed as follows:

ARTICLE I

The Parties undertake, as set forth in the Charter of the United Nations, to settle any international dispute in which they may be involved by peaceful means in such a manner that international peace, security and justice are not endangered and to refrain in their international relations from the threat or use of force in any manner inconsistent with the purposes of the United Nations.

ARTICLE II

In order more effectively to achieve the objective of this Treaty, the Parties separately and jointly by self-help and mutual aid will maintain and develop their individual and collective capacity to resist armed attack and communist subversive activities directed from without against their territorial integrity and political stability.

ARTICLE III

The Parties undertake to strengthen their free institutions and to cooperate with each other in the development of economic progress and social well-being and to further their individual and collective efforts toward these ends.

ARTICLE IV

The Parties, through their Foreign Ministers or their deputies, will consult together from time to time regarding the implementation of this Treaty.

ARTICLE V

Each Party recognizes that an armed attack in the West Pacific Area directed against the territories of either of the Parties would be dangerous to its own peace and safety and declares that it would act to meet the common danger in accordance with its constitutional processes.

Any such armed attack and all measures taken as a result thereof shall be immediately reported to the Security Council of the United Nations. Such measures shall be terminated when the Security Council has taken the measures necessary to restore and maintain international peace and security.

ARTICLE VI

For the purposes of Articles II and V, the terms "territorial" and "territories" shall mean in respect of the Republic of China, Taiwan and the Pescadores; and in respect of the United States of America, the island territories in the West Pacific under its jurisdiction. The provisions of Articles II and V will be applicable to such other territories as may be determined by mutual agreement.

ARTICLE VII

The Government of the Republic of China grants, and the Government of the United States of America accepts, the right to dispose such United States land, air and sea forces in and about Taiwan and the Pescadores as may be required for their defense, as determined by mutual agreement.

ARTICLE VIII

This Treaty does not affect and shall not be interpreted as affecting in any way the rights and obligations of the Parties under the Charter of the United Nations or the responsibility of the United Nations for the maintenance of international peace and security.

ARTICLE IX

This Treaty shall be ratified by the United States of America and the Republic of China in accordance with their respective constitutional processes and will come into force when instruments of ratification thereof have been exchanged by them at Taipei.

ARTICLE X

This Treaty shall remain in force indefinitely. Either Party may terminate it one year after notice has been given to the other Party.

IN WITNESS WHEREOF the undersigned Plenipotentiaries have signed this Treaty.

DONE in duplicate, in the English and Chinese languages, at Washington on this second day of December of the Year One Thousand Nine Hundred and Fifty-four, corresponding to the second day of the twelfth month of the Forty-third year of the Republic of China.

For the United States of America:
JOHN FOSTER DULLES
For the Republic of China:
GEORGE K. C. YEH

Appendix B
THE SHANGHAI COMMUNIQUE (1972)

President Richard Nixon of the United States of America visited the People's Republic of China at the invitation of Premier Chou En-lai of the People's Republic of China from February 21 to February 28, 1972. Accompanying the President were Mrs. Nixon, U.S. Secretary of State William Rogers, Assistant to the President Dr. Henry Kissinger, and other American officials.

President Nixon met with Chairman Mao Tse-tung of the Communist Party of China on February 21. The two leaders had a serious and frank exchange of views on Sino-US relations and world affairs.

During the visit, extensive, earnest and frank discussions were held between President Nixon and Premier Chou En-lai on the normalization of relations between the United States of America and the People's Republic of China, as well as on other matters of interest to both sides. In addition, Secretary of State William Rogers and Foreign Minister Chi Peng-fei held talks in the same spirit.

President Nixon and his party visited Peking and viewed cultural, industrial and agricultural sites, and they also toured Hangchow and Shanghai where, continuing discussions with Chinese leaders, they viewed similar places of interest.

The leaders of the People's Republic of China and the United States of America found it beneficial to have this opportunity, after so many years without contact, to present candidly to one another their views on a variety of issues. They reviewed the international situation in which important changes and great upheavals are taking place and expounded their respective positions and attitudes.

The U.S. side stated: Peace in Asia and peace in the world requires efforts both to reduce immediate tensions and to eliminate the basic causes of conflict. The United States will work for a just and secure peace: just, because it fulfills the aspirations of peoples and nations for freedom and progress; secure, because it removes the danger of foreign aggression. The United States supports individual freedom and social progress for all the peoples of the world, free of outside pressure or intervention. The United States believes that the effort to reduce tensions is served by improving communication between countries that have different ideologies so as to lessen the risks of confrontation through accident, miscalculation or misunderstanding. Countries should treat each other with mutual respect and be willing to compete peacefully, letting performance be the ultimate judge. No country should claim infallibility and each country should be prepared to re-examine its own attitudes for the common good. The United States stressed that the peoples of Indochina should be allowed to determine their destiny without outside intervention; its constant primary objective has been a negotiated solution; the eight-point proposal put forward by the Republic of Vietnam and the United States on January 27, 1972 represents a basis for the attainment of that objective; in the absence of a negotiated settlement the United States envisages the ultimate withdrawal of all U.S. forces from the region consistent with the aim of self-determination for each country of Indochina. The United States will maintain its close ties with and support for the Republic of Korea; the United States will support efforts of the Republic of Korea to seek a relaxation of tension and increased communication in the Korean peninsula. The United States places the highest value on its friendly relations with Japan; it will continue to develop the existing close bonds. Consistent with the United Nations Security Council Resolution of December 21, 1971, the United States favors the continuation of the ceasefire between India and Pakistan and the withdrawal of all military forces to within their own territories and to their own sides of the ceasefire line in Jammu and Kashmir; the United States supports the right of the peoples of South Asia to shape their own future in peace, free of military threat, and without having the area become the subject of great power rivalry.

The Chinese side stated: Wherever there is oppression, there is resistance. Countries want independence, nations want liberation and the people want revolution—this has become the irresistible trend of history. All nations, big or small, should be equal; big nations should not bully the small and strong nations should not bully the weak. China will never be a superpower and it opposes hegemony and power politics of any kind. The Chinese side stated that it firmly supports the struggles of all the oppressed people and nations for freedom and liberation and that the people of all countries have the right to choose their social systems according to their own wishes and the right to safeguard the independence, sovereignty and territorial integrity of their own countries and oppose foreign aggression, interference, control and subversion. All foreign troops should be withdrawn to their own countries.

The Chinese side expressed its firm support to the peoples of Vietnam, Laos and Cambodia in their efforts for the attainment of their goal and its firm support to the seven-point proposal of the Provisional Revolutionary Government of the Republic of South Vietnam and the elaboration of February this year on the two key problems in the proposal, and to the Joint Declaration of the Summit Conference of the Indochinese Peoples. It firmly supports the eight-point program for the peaceful unification of Korea put forward by the Government of the Democratic People's Republic of Korea on April 12, 1971, and the stand for the abolition of the "U.N. Commission for the Unification and Rehabilitation of Korea." It firmly opposes the revival and outward expansion of Japanese militarism and firmly supports the Japanese people's desire to build an independent, democratic, peaceful and neutral Japan. It firmly maintains that India and Pakistan should, in accordance with the United Nations resolutions on the India-Pakistan question, immediately withdraw all their forces to their respective territories and to their own sides of the ceasefire line in Jammu and Kashmir and firmly supports the Pakistan Government and people in their struggle to preserve their independence and sovereignty and the people of Jammu and Kashmir in their struggle for the right of self-determination.

There are essential differences between China and the United States in their social systems and foreign policies. However, the two sides agreed that countries, regardless of their social systems, should conduct their relations on the principles of respect for the sovereignty and territorial integrity of all states, non-aggression against other states, non-interference in the internal affairs of other states, equality and mutual benefit, and peaceful coexistence. International disputes should be settled on this basis, without resorting to the use or threat of force. The United States and the People's Republic of China are prepared to apply these principles to their mutual relations.

With these principles of international relations in mind the two sides stated that:

—progress toward the normalization of relations between China and the United States is in the interests of all countries;

—both wish to reduce the danger of international military conflict;

—neither should seek hegemony in the Asia-Pacific region and each is opposed to efforts by any other country or group of countries to establish such hegemony; and

—neither is prepared to negotiate on behalf of any third party or to enter into agreements or understandings with the other directed at other states.

Both sides are of the view that it would be against the interests of the peoples of the world for any major country to collude with another against other countries, or for major countries to divide up the world into spheres of interest.

The two sides reviewed the long-standing serious disputes between China and the United States. The Chinese side reaffirmed its position: The Taiwan question is the crucial question obstructing the normalization of relations between China and the United States; the Government of the People's Republic of China is the sole legal government of China; Taiwan is a province of China which has long been returned to the motherland; the liberation of Taiwan is China's internal affair in which no other country has the right to interfere; and all U.S. forces and military installations must be withdrawn from Taiwan. The Chinese Government firmly opposes any activities which aim at the creation of "one China, one Taiwan," "one China, two governments," "two Chinas," and "independent Taiwan" or advocate that "the status of Taiwan remains to be determined."

The U.S. side declared: The United States acknowledges that all Chinese on either side of the Taiwan Strait maintain there is but one China and that Taiwan is a part of China. The United States Government does not challenge that position. It reaffirms its interest in a peaceful settlement of the Taiwan question by the Chinese themselves. With this prospect in mind, it affirms the ultimate objective of the withdrawal of all U.S. forces and military installations from Taiwan. In the meantime, it will progressively reduce its forces and military installations on Taiwan as the tension in the area diminishes.

The two sides agreed that it is desirable to broaden the understanding between the two peoples. To this end, they discussed specific areas in such fields as science, technology, culture, sports and journalism, in which people-to-people contacts and exchanges would be mutually beneficial. Each side undertakes to facilitate the further development of such contacts and exchanges.

Both sides view bilateral trade as another area from which mutual benefit can be derived, and agreed that economic relations based on equality and mutual benefit are in the interest of the peoples of the two countries. They agree to facilitate the progressive development of trade between their two countries.

The two sides agreed that they will stay in contact through various channels, including the sending of a senior U.S. representative to Peking from time to time for concrete consultations to further the normalization of relations between the two countries and continue to exchange views on issues of common interest.

The two sides expressed the hope that the gains achieved during this visit would open up new prospects for the relations between the two countries. They believe that the normalization of relations between the two countries is not only in the interest of the Chinese and American peoples but also contributes to the relaxation of tension in Asia and the world.

President Nixon, Mrs. Nixon and the American party expressed their appreciation for the gracious hospitality shown them by the Government and people of the People's Republic of China.

Appendix C
JOINT COMMUNIQUE ON THE ESTABLISHMENT OF DIPLOMATIC RELATIONS BETWEEN THE UNITED STATES AND THE PEOPLE'S REPUBLIC OF CHINA (1978)

The United States of America and the People's Republic of China have agreed to recognize each other and to establish diplomatic relations as of Jan. 1, 1979.

The United States of America recognizes the Government of the People's Republic of China as the sole legal Government of China. Within this context, the people of the United States will maintain cultural, commercial and other unofficial relations with the people of Taiwan.

The United States of America and the People's Republic of China reaffirm the principles agreed on by the two sides in the Shanghai Communique and emphasize once again that:

• Both wish to reduce the danger of international military conflict.

• Neither should seek hegemony in the Asia-Pacific region or in any other region of the world and each is opposed to efforts by any other country or group of countries to establish such hegemony.

• Neither is prepared to negotiate on behalf of any third party or to enter into agreements or understandings with the other directed at other states.

• The United States of America acknowledges the Chinese position that there is but one China and Taiwan is part of China.

• Both believe that normalization of Sino-American relations is not only in the interest of the Chinese and American peoples but also contributes to the cause of peace in Asia and the world.

The United States of America and the People's Republic of China will exchange ambassadors and establish embassies on March 1, 1979.

NOTES

Introduction

1. See Address to Foreign Policy Association, June 23, 1976, for Carter's views on the appropriate diplomatic style.

2. *Philadelphia Inquirer*, February 10, 1979.

Chapter One

1. Ruth L. Sivard, *World Military and Social Expenditures, 1976* (Leesburg, Virginia: WMSE Publications, 1976). The *Far Eastern Economic Review*, May 7, 1976, puts China below Iran; most other authoritative sources give a range estimate of China's defense expenditures making it possible to rank China from third to sixth in the world.

2. *New York Times* (Week in Review), January 7, 1979.

3. David Rees, "The Gorshkov Strategy in the Far East," *Pacific Community*, January 1978, pp. 143-155.

4. *New York Times*, November 12, 1978.

5. *Time*, February 5, 1979, p. 32.

6. *London Observer*, November 12, 1978.

7. *New York Times*, February 10, 1979.

8. *Christian Science Monitor,* July 20, 1978.

9. Robert A. Scalapino, *Asia and the Road Ahead* (Berkeley: University of California Press, 1975), p. 177.

10. Department of Defense, *Annual Report, Fiscal Year 1980* (Harold Brown, Secretary of Defense), p. 105.

11. Moscow Radio in Korean, January 5, 1979, in FBIS, *Daily Report* (USSR), January 8, 1979, pp. M1-2.

12. *Far Eastern Economic Review,* November 3, 1978, p. 7.

13. A. Doak Barnett, *China Policy* (Washington: Brookings, 1977), pp. 88-89.

14. Japan has already embarked on new defense plans and has not been so shy about announcing its intent to rearm. For example, recently the Japanese Prime Minister, for the first time since World War II, brought defense issues to the Diet. For further details, see Michael Pillsbury, "Playing the Japanese Card," *Foreign Policy,* Winter 1978-1979.

15. KYODO (Tokyo) in English, December 23, 1978, in FBIS, *Daily Report* (Asia and Pacific), December 26, 1978, p. C4.

16. *New York Times,* February 10, 1979.

17. *Ibid.,* February 8, 1979.

Chapter Two

1. *Washington Post,* December 21, 1978.

2. *Ibid.*

3. Neil H. Jacoby, *U.S. Aid to Taiwan: A Study of Foreign Aid, Self-Help and Development* (New York: Praeger, 1966), p. 35.

4. *Ibid.*, p. 11.

5. *Ibid.*, p. 165.

6. *Ibid.*, p. 172. The late governor of Taiwan, Chen Cheng, is known as the "father" of Taiwan's land reform program. Nevertheless, according to Jacoby, American personnel of the Joint Commission on Rural Reconstruction were instrumental in planning the program and in its implementation.

7. Anthony Y. C. Koo, "Economic Development of Taiwan," in Paul K. T. Shih, ed., *Taiwan in Modern Times* (New York: St. John's University Press, 1973), p. 413.

8. *Ibid.*

9. According to PRC sources, the land reform program of the early 1950s "eliminated" 10 million landlords. This does not include the land owners killed during World War II or in the civil war that followed.

10. Koo, "Economic Development of Taiwan," p. 418.

11. Kung-chia Yeh, "Economic Growth: An Overview," in Yuan-li Wu and Kung-chia Yen, eds., *Growth Distribution and Social Change: Essays on the Republic of China* (University of Maryland School of Law, Occasional Papers/Reprint Series in Contemporary Asian Studies, no. 3, 1978). p. 14.

12. *Ibid.*

13. The above-cited statistics come from *National Conditions* (Taipei: Statistical Bureau of the Executive Yuan, Winter 1977).

14. See *Encyclopedia Britannica Yearbook* (1977), p. 498.

15. The *New York Times*, April 2, 1977, states that Taiwan's income differentiation is less than in the United States or Japan. For further details, see Yuan-li Wu, "Income Distribution in the Process of Economic Growth," in Wu and Yeh, eds., *Growth From Below: A People-Oriented Development Strategy* (Washington: Overseas Development Council, December 1973), p. 23. See Jan S. Prybyla, "Economic Developments in Taiwan," in Hungdah Chiu, ed., *China and the Taiwan Issue: Problems, Analysis and Documents* (New York: Praeger, forth-

coming) for details on the argument that Taiwan's income spread between rich and poor is less than China's.

16. As of August 1977, U.S. private investment in Taiwan amounted to $508 million. See statement by Marinus Van Gessel, President of the American Chamber of Commerce in Taiwan, in *Normalization of Relations with the People's Republic of China: Practical Implications,* Hearings before the Subcommittee on Asian and Pacific Affairs, Committee on International Relations, 95th Congress, September-October 1977.

17. For details on the ten projects, see *Asian Wall Street Journal,* July 13, 1978. The shipbuilding plant and the steel complex were the most highly questioned of the projects at the onset. The re-evaluation of the Japanese yen, which caused the price of Japanese steel to escalate, had indirectly made the steel mill more profitable. Currently, the shipbuilding yard and the petrochemical complex seem least likely to be profitable. For further details on the argument that the ROC undertook the projects largely for political reasons, see John F. Copper, "Taiwan's Strategy and America's China Policy," ORBIS, Summer 1977.

18. For further details, see the *New York Times,* July 4, 1976.

19. *China Yearbook, 1964-1965* (Taipei: Chinese Publishing Co., 1965), pp. 402-403.

20. These figures can be found in various issues of the *New York Times.*

21. Far Eastern Economic Review, *Asia 1978 Yearbook,* p. 318. In the first half of 1978, the figure was 41 per cent; see *Asian Wall Street Journal,* September 29, 1978.

22. Ralph N. Clough, *Island China* (Cambridge: Harvard University Press, 1978), p. 77. By 1978, only 22.7 per cent of industrial production was government-operated.

23. Gene Gregory, "The New Prosperity: Towards an Asian Common Market," *Far Eastern Economic Review,* October 13, 1978.

24. Central Intelligence Agency, *Handbook of Economic Statistics,* September 1977, p. 1.

25. John P. Hardt, "Summary," in *China: A Reassessment of the Economy,* A Compendium of Papers Submitted to the Economic Committee, Congress of the United States, July 10, 1975, p. 12.

26. Far Eastern Economic Review, *Asia 1978 Yearbook,* p. 168. Figures are based on Citibank estimates.

27. See William A. Sullivan, "The Chinese Connection, 1789-1937," in William W. Whitson, ed., *Doing Business with China: American Trade Opportunities in the 1970s* (New York: Praeger, 1974), pp. 3-13.

28. Dwight H. Perkins, "Is There a China Market?" in Whitson, ed., *Doing Business with China,* p. 49.

29. S. H. Chan, "The Pattern of China's Trade," *Current History,* September 1978. U.S.-PRC trade in 1978 was approximately $1 billion, but a large portion of this was not accounted for.

30. See Alexander Eckstein, "Sino-American Economic Relations," in William J. Barnds, ed., *China and America: The Search for a New Relationship* (New York: New York University Press, 1977).

31. *Red Flag* (Peking), April 1976.

32. For a more complete discussion of the Chinese products that can most likely find a market in the United States in the immediate future, see Eckstein, "Sino-American Economic Relations."

33. This problem is discussed in Joey Bonner and Howard J. Kaufman, "Control of Imports: Attitudes of American Labor," in Whitson, ed., *Doing Business with China,* pp. 116-125.

34. Perkins, "Is there a China Market?" p. 47.

35. *Ibid.,* p. 45.

36. Japan, South Korea and a number of Southeast Asian countries have expressed their concern with United States weapons and computer sales to China. Moscow has also accused the United States of not adhering to its equidistance policy by selling things to China it does not sell to the Soviet Union or things the Soviet Union does not need. There have also been complaints by Congressmen and citizen groups in the United States regarding the sale of weapons-related technology to China.

37. For further details on this point, see Harold C. Hinton, "Will Politics Govern China's Trade with America?" in Whitson, ed., *Doing Business with China*, pp. 13-26. It is also worth noting that China has done the same for the Soviet Union recently and that the Kremlin became more serious in negotiating their border problems.

38. U.S. statute defines recipients of MFN treatment as "political entit[ies] known as nation[s]." The Japanese accord Taiwan MFN status simply by putting "Taiwan" in column one for nondiscriminating tariffs, but their method obviously does not apply to the United States.

39. *New York Times*, January 16, 1979.

40. See Victor H. Li, *De-recognizing Taiwan: The Legal Problems* (Washington: Carnegie Endowment, 1977), pp. 21-22.

41. For further details, *ibid*.

42. On the above, see Eugene A. Theroux, "Normalization and Some Practical and Legal Problems Concerning the United States," in Hungdah Chiu, ed., *Normalizing Relations with the People's Republic of China: Problems, Analysis and Documents* (University of Maryland Law School, Occasional Papers/Reprint Series in Contemporary Asian Studies, no. 2, 1978), pp. 81-82.

Chapter Three

1. Eleanor C. McDowell, *Digest of United States Practice in International Law, 1976* (Washington: GPO, 1977), p. 1. This quote is taken from a speech given by President Ford on October 21, 1976, when he signed the Foreign Sovereign Immunities Act of 1976.

2. The Chinese rendering of "does not challenge" was *wu yi yi*, which would probably be better translated as "being generally in agreement since there is no disagreement." For further details on the language and other problems in this document, see John F. Copper, "Reassessing the Shanghai Communique," *The Asian Wall Street Journal*, December 27, 1977. Many simplistic conclusions have been drawn by Ameri-

can observers; as one example, note the language of a *New York Times* editorial, February 11, 1979: "What it [the Congress] should not do is undermine the deal by destroying its central element: American recognition, since 1972, that Taiwan belongs to China." The central question is much more open than the editorial writers acknowledge.

3. See "U.S. Foreign Policy for the 1970s: The Emerging Structure of Peace, A Report to the Congress by Richard Nixon," in *Department of State Bulletin,* March 13, 1972, p. 330.

4. "President Nixon's Visit to the PRC, News Conference of Dr. Kissinger and Mr. Green," *ibid.,* p. 428.

5. For further information on Taiwan's tributary status, see John K. Fairbank, ed., *The Chinese World Order: Traditional China's Foreign Relations* (Cambridge: Harvard University Press, 1968).

6. It is also worthy of note that much of Taiwan today is still not populated by Chinese and that even under Japanese control (1895-1945) the aborigines controlled much of the inner part of the island to the point that neither Chinese nor Japanese went there, or did so at considerable risk.

7. Sophia Su-fei Yen, *Taiwan in China's Foreign Relations, 1836-1874* (Hamden, Conn.: Shoestring Press, 1965), pp. 136-139.

8. E. House, *The Japanese Expedition to Formosa;* cited in Lung-chu Chen and W. M. Reisman, "Who Owns Taiwan: A Search for International Title," in Yung-hwan Jo, ed., *Taiwan's Future* (Hong Kong: Union Research Institute, 1974), p. 174.

9. Chen and Reisman, "Who Owns Taiwan," p. 174.

10. George W. Barclay, *Colonial Development and Population in Taiwan* (Port Washington, N.Y.: Kennikat Press, 1954), p. 33.

11. See George H. Kerr, *Formosa Betrayed* (Boston: Houghton Mifflin, 1965), p. 31.

12. See, for example, Winston S. Churchill, *Memoirs of the Second World War* (Boston: Houghton Mifflin, 1959), p. 753.

13. For further details, see Wolf Mendl, *Issues in Japan's China Policy* (New York: Oxford University Press, 1978), p. 13.

14. Edgar Snow, *Red Star over China* (New York: Random House, 1938), pp. 88-89.

15. *Department of State Bulletin*, no. 79, 1950.

16. *Ibid.*, no. 896, 1954.

17. Stanley Karnow, "Our Next Move on China," *New York Times Magazine*, August 14, 1977, p. 34.

18. *Mainichi Daily News* (Tokyo), March 29, 1972.

19. In late 1954 and early 1955, the PRC bombarded the Ta Chen Islands, islets north of the other off-shore islands. It subsequently executed a successful amphibious assault on Ichiang Shan, one of the islets to the north of the main group. The ROC, following U.S. advice, subsequently withdrew from the rest of the Ta Chens. With this exception, the ROC has not experienced any territorial losses.

20. The *New York Times*, November 21, 1977, cites a figure of 60 per cent; the *Far Eastern Economic Review*, December 3, 1976, states that it is 70 per cent, but on August 8, 1975, says it may be as high as 80 per cent.

21. Clough, *Island China*, pp. 135-146.

22. The KMT's membership in 1976 was over 1.5 million, which was about 10 per cent of the population. Membership in the Communist Party in the PRC is around 2 per cent of the population.

23. Gerald McBeath, "Taiwan in 1977: Holding the Reins," *Asian Survey*, January 1978.

24. See Clough, *Island China*, pp. 155-160, for details.

25. *Ibid.*, p. 161.

26. *Ibid.*, pp. 161-168, for further details.

27. Rosalyn Higgins, *The Development of International Law Through the Political Organs of the United Nations* (London: Oxford University Press, 1963), pp. 54-55.

Chapter Four

1. *New York Times,* December 18, 1978.

2. *Ibid.,* December 25, 1978.

3. *Ibid.,* January 10, 1979.

4. *U.S. News & World Report,* December 4, 1978.

5. See Article XIV of the PRC Constitution of 1975 and Article XVIII of the 1978 Constitution.

6. Mao Tse-tung, "On People's Democratic Dictatorship," in *Selected Works of Mao,* vol. 4, (Peking: Foreign Languages Press, 1961), p. 418.

7. *Kuang Ming Jih Pao* (Peking), November 2, 1978.

8. *Political Imprisonment in the People's Republic of China,* An Amnesty International Report, 1978, p. xi.

9. See, also, *New York Times,* November 28, 1978.

10. Raymond D. Gastil, *Freedom in the World* (New York: Freedom House, 1978), p. 240.

11. Testimony of Richard L. Walker, in U.S. Congress, Senate Subcommittee on Internal Security, Committee on the Judiciary, *Report on Figures of Human Lives Killed by Peking Regime,* 92nd Congress, 1st Session, August 12, 1971.

12. Simon Leys, "Human Rights in China," *National Review,* December 8, 1978, p. 1541.

13. *Washington Post,* August 8, 1973.

14. Bruce J. Esposito, "The Cultural Revolution and China's Scientific Establishment," *Current Scene,* August 1974.

15. Fred Coleman, "China Alters Course," *Newsweek,* October 30, 1978.

16. Mab Huang, "Human Rights in a Revolutionary Setting," paper presented at the International Studies Annual Convention, St. Louis, March 1977.

17. Leys, "Human Rights in China," p. 1544.

18. Testimony of Burton Levin, in U.S. Congress, House Subcommittee on International Organizations, Committee on International Relations, *Human Rights in Taiwan,* 95th Congress, 1st Session, June 14, 1977.

19. *New York Times,* December 26, 1976.

20. Burton Levin (see fn. 18, above).

21. Miss Chen was found in possession of "illegal materials." This could have been very serious several years ago. But, instead of receiving punishment, she was just detained for a few days of questioning and "re-education."

22. Levin (see fn. 18, above).

23. Hart Clifton, "Freedom Limited in Taiwan," *San Mateo Times,* February 10, 1978.

24. *Ming Pao Monthly* (Hong Kong), July 1978, p. 17.

25. *Far Eastern Economic Review,* December 22, 1978, p. 22.

26. Smith Hempstone, "Taiwan's Anxious Boom," *Washington Post,* July 23, 1978.

27. *New York Times,* April 12, 1977.

28. Donald Zagoria, "Normalizing Relations with China Without 'Abandoning' Taiwan," *Pacific Community,* October 1977. p. 74.

29. Gastil, *Freedom in the World,* p. 240.

30. *Ibid.,* p. 239.

31. *Central Daily News* (Taipei), December 17, 1978.

32. See *Far Eastern Economic Review,* February 2, 1979, p. 15.

Chapter Five

1. By the late 1960s, the Kuomintang (Nationalist Party) had become more than 50 per cent Taiwanese. At present, it is between 60 and 80 per cent Taiwanese. See the *New York Times*, November 21, 1977, which cites the figure 60 per cent, and the *Far Eastern Economic Review*, December 3, 1976, and August 8, 1975, for figures of 70 and 80 per cent, respectively.

2. President Ford promised the ROC self-sufficiency in weapons and during his tenure in office sold Taipei a $34-million air-defense system, a battalion of Hawk surface-to-air missiles, and the right to build 60 more F5E fighter aircraft in addition to helicopters and other small arms. See the *New York Times*, April 6, 1977.

3. This conference was held on May 12, and the interpretation given here was made both in the United States and Taiwan. See, for example, *United Daily News* (Taipei), May 13, 1977.

4. For an analysis of U.S. public opinion toward the PRC and the ROC, see Michael Yin-mao Kao *et al.*, "Public Opinion and U.S. China policy," in Chiu, ed., *Normalizing Relations with the People's Republic of China.*

5. *Ibid.* This is based on Gallup polls.

6. "Great Decisions '76 Opinion Ballots," Foreign Policy Association News Release, June 30, 1976.

7. Cited in *Asian Mail*, July 1977.

8. The results of this poll were released on September 11, 1978, and were cited in several U.S. newspapers.

9. Kao *et al.*, "Public Opinion and U.S. China Policy," in Chiu, ed., *Normalizing Relations with the People's Republic of China*, p. 89.

10. Further see Clough, *Island China*, p. 211.

11. Stephen Barber, "The Senate Stays Loyal," *Far Eastern Economic Review*, October 27, 1978.

12. *Ibid.*

13. For more details, see Robert G. Sutter, *Chinese Foreign Policy after the Cultural Revolution, 1966-1977* (Boulder: Westview Press, 1978), pp. 105-113.

14. See the *New York Times*, February 18, 1978.

15. Some observers contend that ROC leaders would be extremely reluctant to declare their independence because of the fact that changing the name of the country would provoke the Taiwanese to ask for proportional representation or to rally against the Mainlander-dominated government. On the other hand, it appears that Mainland-Taiwanese differences are no longer so acute. In the event of an external threat from the PRC, they would surely unify. Evidence that the latter view is a perception in Taipei includes the fact that a number of close ROC friends in the United States have publicly advocated that a plebiscite be used to resolve the "Taiwan question."

16. See John W. Garver, "Taiwan's Russian Option," *Asian Survey,* July 1978, p. 755.

17. This was picked up and criticized by the PRC. See New China News Agency, January 10, 1970.

18. See, for example, the *New York Times*, March 8, 1972; the *Washington Post*, May 14, 1973; and *Far Eastern Economic Review,* June 27, 1975.

19. Garver, "Taiwan's Russian Option," p. 755.

20. Harold Hinton, *The Sino-Soviet Confrontation: Implications for the Future* (New York: National Strategic Information Center, 1977), p. 28.

21. Garver, "Taiwan's Russian Option," p. 756.

22. FBIS, *Daily Report,* August 1, 1978.

23. *China News* (Taipei), March 9, 1972.

24. *New York Times*, April 1 and July 19, 1978.

25. Clough, *Island China,* p. 117.

26. Melinda Liu, "Accounting for the N-factor," *Far Eastern Economic Review,* December 17, 1976.

27. Melinda Liu, "Taipei Treads Lightly," *ibid.,* January 6, 1978.

28. Liu, "Accounting for the N-factor."

29. *Washington Post,* August 29, 1976.

30. *Keesing's Contemporary Archives,* February 25, 1977.

31. Melinda Liu, "Israel Fills Nationalists' Arms Gap," *Far Eastern Economic Review,* April 29, 1977.

32. See the *Far Eastern Economic Review,* October 20, 1978.

Chapter Six

1. *Central Daily News* (Taipei), December 28, 1978.

2. *Far Eastern Economic Review,* January 12, 1979, p. 22.

3. *Ibid.,* p. 23.

MONOGRAPHS from the Foreign Policy Research Institute

"... distinguished essays on many of the hottest foreign policy issues."

—National Review

Broker or Advocate?
The U.S. Role in the Arab-Israeli Dispute, 1973-1978

HARVEY SICHERMAN

An absorbing narrative of the principal events and an evaluation of the successes and failures of two diplomatic styles: Kissinger's "brokerage" and Carter's "advocacy." Puts the Camp David summit in perspective.

1978, 120 pp., $4.00

"Finlandization": A Map to a Metaphor

ADAM M. GARFINKLE

1978, 56 pp., $4.00

Southern Africa in the World: Autonomy or Interdependence?

RICHARD E. BISSELL

1978, 67 pp., $4.00

Defense Manpower Policy: A Critical Reappraisal

ALAN NED SABROSKY

1978, 107 pp., tables, $4.00

The above monographs may be ordered from FPRI, 3508 Market St., Suite 350, Philadelphia, PA 19104.